GW01006155

100 FACTS

West Ham

First published in Great Britain in 2018
by Wymer Publishing
www.wymerpublishing.co.uk
Wymer Publishing is a trading name of Wymer (UK) Ltd

ISBN 978-1-908724-80-9

Edited by Jerry Bloom.

Typeset by The Andys.
Printed and bound by Clays, Bungay, Suffolk

A catalogue record for this book is available from the British Library.

Cover design by The Andys.
Sketches by Becky Welton. © 2014.

West Ham

Steve Horton

1895
THAMES IRONWORKS

FACT 1

The club that became West Ham United were founded in 1895 by the Thames Ironworks & Shipbuilding Company.

Foreman Dave Taylor, who was also a football referee, was the instigator of the club. He approached company owner Arnold Hills who agreed to provide financial backing. The formation of the club was announced in the company's weekly journal on 29th June 1895.

Taylor organised fixtures but then handed over the running of the club to Ted Harsent, who became the first secretary. He arranged for home games to be played at Hermit Road in Canning Town, the previous home of Old Castle Swifts who folded that summer. The club colours were Oxford blue, in honour of where Hills went to university.

The first game was a friendly against Royal Ordnance reserves on 7th September. This ended in a 0-0 draw and three weeks later they beat Manor Park 8-0. However there was no luck in the FA Cup when they were drawn away to Chatham and lost 5-0 in Kent.

Over the course of the season Thames Ironworks played 47 games, most of them friendlies. They won 30, drew 5 and lost 12.

FACT 2

1896 WEST HAM CHARITY CUP

Thames Ironworks won a trophy in their first season when they lifted the West Ham Charity Cup.

The cup was inaugurated in 1888 and involved teams from the West Ham and surrounding area in what was then the county of Essex.

In the semi-final Thames Ironworks beat Park Grove 3-0 to set up a final with Barking. This was played on 21st March at the Spotted Dog ground in Upton Lane and ended 2-2.

The replay a week later was drawn 0-0, leading to a third game being played at Beckton Road on 20th April. In front of what the *Evening Standard* described as 'good company' both sides were reduced to ten men through injury.

Late in the game Billy Barnes scored the winning goal for the Ironworkers. Barnes was still a few weeks short of his seventeenth birthday. He would later gain fame when he scored the winner for Sheffield United in the 1902 FA Cup final.

The following season Thames Ironworks again reached the final but this time they were on the losing side. After beating Manor Park in the semi-final, they were beaten 1-0 by Garfield.

FACT 3

1897
TWO NEW GROUNDS

After being evicted from their Hermit Road ground, Thames Ironworks twice moved into new homes in 1897.

The club were given an eviction notice by their landlords in October 1896 and had to play games on opponents grounds. Arnold Hills managed to lease some land off Browning Road in East Ham and on 6th March 1897 the Ironworks played their first game there, beating Ilford 3-2.

Browning Road was not in an ideal location and didn't prove popular with supporters. Just a month later Ironworks drew 1-1 against Barking Woodville in what turned out to be their last game at the ground.

Hills identified another site in Canning Town and spent £20,000 building the Memorial Grounds. As well as the football pitch there was a cycle track, tennis courts and swimming pool. Hills also persuaded the London, Tilbury & Southend Railway to build a station at the site.

It was estimated the the ground could hold up to 100,000 but the attendance for the first football fixture there was much lower. Around 2,000 spectators turned up to see the Ironworks beat Brentford 1-0 on 11th September in the London League.

FACT 4

1898
LONDON LEAGUE CHAMPIONS

Thames Ironworks were champions of the London League in 1897-98, only the second season the club had entered the competition.

The Ironworkers were runners up in 1896-97 and prior to the following campaign had secured the Memorial Grounds, meaning they had a proper ground to call home.

After beating Brentford at home in the first game of the season, the Ironworkers won their next five matches. One of these was 1-0 away at champions 3rd Grenadier Guards, a victory that gave them a great sense of self belief.

By the turn of the year Thames Ironworks were top of the league and still hadn't lost a game. They continued to avoid defeat and on 15th January came out the best in a ten goal spectacular, winning 7-3 at Bromley.

They remained unbeaten until the penultimate game, but a 1-0 defeat at Brentford saw them fall below the Bees in the table. However the following week the Ironworkers won at 2nd Grenadier Guards while Brentford lost against Barking Woodville.

Thames Ironworks won the league with a 100% home record and had also scored the most goals and had the meanest defence.

1898
TURNING PROFESSIONAL

FACT 5

After winning the London League, Thames Ironworks switched from amateur to professional status and joined the Southern League.

The Ironworkers were now able to bring in players from other London clubs and strengthened the side in defence and attack. They also signed keeper Tommy Moore from Millwall Athletic, a move that infuriated their rivals.

The first Southern League game was a 3-0 win at Shepherds Bush and they went on to lose just once all season. That defeat was a 4-1 loss at Wycombe, when the players plans had been disrupted due to missing the train. Ironically Wycombe missed their train for the return fixture and themselves suffered a 4-1 defeat.

The biggest win of the season was a 10-0 thrashing of Maidenhead in the last game at the Memorial Grounds. Despite winning the second division of the league by nine points, the Ironworkers then had to play some test matches to determine whether or not they would be promoted.

Thames Ironworks beat Cowes Sports 3-1 but then drew 1-1 with Sheppey United. However before a replay could take place the top division of the league was enlarged, allowing Thames Ironworks to join it.

FACT 6

1899 THE DEATH OF HARRY BRADSHAW

Thames Ironworks were stunned at Christmas 1899 when they learned of the death of captain Harry Bradshaw.

A former Football League player with Liverpool who also had one England cap, Bradshaw joined the Ironworkers from Tottenham Hotspur in the summer of 1899. He was immediately appointed captain and got

on with everybody, being admired for his clever wing play.

On 9th December he scored in a 2-1 FA Cup defeat against Millwall and picked up a leg injury, ruling him out of games for the next few weeks. On Christmas Day morning Bradshaw watched his teammates face Portsmouth and appeared to be quite well.

After the game Bradshaw returned to his home in Tottenham where he began vomiting and complaining of pains in the chest and head. His wife sent for a doctor but he fitted and died before one arrived.

Bradshaw was just 26 years old and the cause of death was a ruptured blood vessel. His widow Elizabeth revealed that four years earlier he was kicked in the head during a game and suffered discharges from the ears ever since. A doctor confirmed that his death may have been an eventual consequence of this.

The following April a benefit match took place between Thames Ironworks and Tottenham, with all funds going to Bradshaw's widow and two young children.

FACT 7

1900
WEST HAM UNITED

In 1900 Thames Ironworks was wound up and a new club was formed to take their place in the Southern League.

The Ironworkers finished fourteenth out of fifteen teams in their first season in Southern League's top division. They then beat Fulham in a test match to preserve their status.

Off the pitch, Thames Ironworks & Shipbuilding Company took over another engineering firm. This meant a limited company with shareholders was formed, compared to the previous set up of one man owning the whole business.

With some concerns over such a company running a football club, Thames Ironworks resigned from the Southern League at the end of June and ceased to exist. However almost immediately a new club was formed, West Ham United. This was made up of many of the playing and non playing staff from Thames Ironworks including Syd King who would later become manager.

West Ham were offered the Southern League place vacated by the Ironworkers and would play fixtures at the Memorial Grounds. Their first league game under the new guise was on 1st September at home to Gravesend, who were thrashed 7-0 in front of a crowd of 2,000.

1901
TWO GAMES IN ONE DAY

FACT 8

On 2nd November 1901 West Ham took a gamble by playing matches in the Southern League and FA Cup on the same day, fielding two separate teams.

The Hammers were due to face Tottenham at the Memorial Grounds that day in a keenly anticipated derby. However that date was also set aside for FA Cup qualifying fixtures and they had been drawn at home to Leyton.

A Saturday derby with Tottenham, one of the Southern League's top sides and current FA Cup holders, was certain to attract a bigger crowd than a game with Leyton who were in a minor league. To get round the problem, club officials decided to concede home advantage in the cup and play the game at Leyton, sending a reserve side to play the tie.

On the day itself, West Ham were beaten 1-0 by Spurs in front of a huge crowd of 17,000. This was almost double the attendance for any other league fixture at the Memorial Ground that season.

The gamble paid off when it came to the FA Cup too, with a reserve side beating Leyton 1-0. In the following round however the Hammers exited the competition, losing 2-1 at home to Grays before just 2,000 fans.

FACT 9

1902
WEST HAM'S FIRST INTERNATIONAL

The first West Ham player to appear for his country was William Jones, who was selected to play for Wales in the British Championship in 1902.

Born in 1876 in the village of Penrhiwceiber, Jones had already been capped by Wales when he was signed by the Hammers in December 1901. He joined from Kettering in a swap deal that saw Peter Kyle go in the other direction.

A good tackler who could also get the ball forward to the wingers, he played fifteen times in the Southern League that season and was only on the losing side twice.

In March 1902 Jones was called up by Wales for British Championship fixtures against England and Scotland. At Wrexham the game with England was drawn 0-0 but Wales were then hammered 5-1 by Scotland in Greenock.

The game with Scotland turned out to be the last of Jones's four appearances for his country. In the summer of 1902 he returned to his homeland and joined Aberamam Athletic, where he won the Welsh Cup. It was a one sided final in which Wrexham were thrashed 8-0. He died in World War One, killed in action in Macedonia.

FACT 10

1904
THE BOLEYN GROUND/ UPTON PARK

At the start of the 1904-05 season West Ham moved to a ground that would be their home for the next 114 years.

With the lease at the Memorial Grounds up for renewal, the club couldn't reach a new rental agreement and opted to move to the Old Castle Ground in Upton Park. This was situated within the grounds of the Green Street House and had once been a field where cabbages and potatoes were grown. The ground had covered seating on one side, a covered terrace behind one goal and open standing on the other sides.

The name Boleyn Ground was adopted in 1905. This comes from the fact that the house was known locally as the Boleyn Castle. It was believed King Henry VIII's second wife had stayed there at some point, although she was actually beheaded before the house was built. Although the Boleyn Ground remained the official name, it was always commonly known as Upton Park after the area in which it was situated.

The first game there was a Southern League fixture against Millwall on 1st September 1904. Billy Bridgeman scored twice as the Hammers won 3-0 in front of a crowd of 10,000.

FACT 11

1910
CROSSED HAMMERS CREST

The first time that West Ham began adopting a crest with crossed hammers was on match programmes during the 1910-11 season.

The hammers represented the tools used in shipbuilding by the workers of Thames Ironworks. In 1910-11 programme covers began depicting a drawing of a footballer with two crossed hammers situated either side. In the early 1920s programme drawings of a castle were added as well.

After World War Two the blazers of players and officials carried a badge with crossed hammers and a castle on it, separated by WHUFC written in the middle. In 1958, when West Ham were promoted to Division One, the hammers and castle were merged together into the crest for the first time. The new design first appeared on a special handbook costing two shillings.

Apart from the occasional minor change the crest remained the same until 2016, except for the centenary season when two players and '100 years' were superimposed. However after the move from Upton Park the castle was dropped from the crest and 'London' added, as the club sought wider worldwide appeal.

1911
GIANT KILLERS

FACT 12

The Hammers were involved in an act of giant killing in 1911 when they knocked Division One leaders Manchester United out of the FA Cup.

There was no squad rotation in the cups in those days and the visitors were at full strength for the 3rd round tie that took place on 25th February 1911. A crowd of 27,000, including several hundred from

Manchester, crammed into the ground with some up telegraph poles and others on the stand roof.

The visitors were the better side early on but after seventeen minutes West Ham scored with their first attack. George Webb ran past several defenders before passing for Danny Shea to score. Five minutes later Manchester United were level, Sandy Turnbull's header from a corner giving keeper George Kitchen no chance.

In the second half West Ham saw little of the ball but contained the opposition quite easily. With two minutes remaining and a replay looking likely Shea whipped a dangerous ball into the area and Tommy Caldwell scored from close range.

The last few minutes were frantic but West Ham held out for a famous win. The Hammers had now reached the quarter-finals but that was where the tremendous run finally came to an end as they lost 3-2 to Blackburn at Upton Park.

FACT 13

1914
THE WEST HAM PALS

The outbreak of war in 1914 led to the suspension of national football competition and the formation of a special band of servicemen.

Britain declared war on Germany on 6th August 1914 and men immediately began volunteering to join the armed forces. The following month author Arthur Conan Doyle called for players to join up and a

football battalion was formed as part of the Middlesex Regiment.

The football battalion was commanded by Frank Buckley, who played for Bradford City. It was estimated that 40% of England's 5,000 professional footballers joined up and that of the first 600 in the football battalion, 500 were killed in action.

The 13th battalion of the Essex Regiment was known as the West Ham Pals. This was made up of Thames Ironworks workers and supporters of the football club. The regiment's battle cry was 'Up the Hammers' and they fought in some of World War One's bloodiest battles.

Over 1,000 servicemen from the West Ham Pals were killed or missing in action. In 2009 a plaque was unveiled at Upton Park by Trevor Brooking to commemorate these brave men.

FACT 14

1918
SYD PUDDEFOOT'S SEVEN GOALS

Striker Syd Puddefoot scored seven times when they thrashed Crystal Palace 11-0 in a wartime fixture.

Organised football was suspended during World War One and small regional competitions took place instead. The Hammers took part in the London Combination, which was formed for the city's clubs in 1915.

The match in which 23 year old Puddefoot scored his seven goals took place at Upton Park on 6th April 1918. It was the last game of the season and the Hammers would win the title if rivals Chelsea slipped up. Despite making no mistakes and winning 11-0, Chelsea beat Clapton Orient 6-1 and the Hammers had to settle for second place.

Puddefoot, who had joined West Ham in 1912, remained with them after the war before moving to Falkirk in 1922. He returned to Upton Park as a 37 year old towards the end of 1931-32 as the Hammers unsuccessfully fought relegation. In his second spell with the club he scored three times in 22 appearances.

After retiring from playing Puddefoot managed both Galatasaray and Fenerbache in Turkey. He died in 1972.

FACT 15

1918
I'M FOREVER BLOWING BUBBLES

'I'm Forever Blowing Bubbles', the song that is most associated with West Ham was first performed in 1918.

Written by John Kellette, which was actually a pseudonym for three writers who worked together, the song was first sung by Helen Carrington in the Broadway musical *The Passing Show* of 1918.

In the 1920s it was performed at music halls across the United Kingdom and it featured in a number of films in the 1930s and 1950s. Nowadays 'Bubbles' is best known as West Ham's anthem, but its exact origins can not be pinpointed.

One theory is that it was connected to club trialist from the early 1920s, Billy 'Bubbles' Murray. Murray's headmaster, was said to have sang Bubbles during a schoolboy game in which he played at Upton Park. The song was then adopted by fans, so the saying goes. It has even been claimed that trainer Charlie Paynter brought in a house band on occasions to play music as the crowd sang along. However there is no conclusive evidence of this and the first time fans are recorded as having sang Bubbles was at the War Cup final in 1940.

One thing that is certain is despite the confusion over the origins, it is now difficult to imagine any West Ham game without 'Bubbles'.

FACT 16

1919
ELECTION TO THE FOOTBALL LEAGUE

When national football competition resumed after the end of World War One, West Ham were elected into the Football League.

For the 1919-20 season the two divisions were expanded from twenty to 22 clubs. At a meeting in Manchester in March 1919, the Hammers were elected along with Coventry City, Rotherham County and South Shields. The club's application to the Football League was a blow to the Southern League, who had seen West Ham as one of their big attractions.

West Ham's first match in Division Two was at home to Lincoln City on 30th August that year. In front of a crowd of 20,000 the visitors' took the lead in the first half from the penalty spot but after the break the Hammers were much improved. James Moyes equalised and even though Alf Lee had to retire through injury the Hammers remained the more likely to score again. In the end though they had to settle for a point.

Two days later the Hammers were thrashed 7-0 at Barnsley. However despite the shaky start they soon found their feet in the Football League and finished a respectable seventh in the final table.

1923
THE WHITE HORSE FINAL

FACT 17

In addition to winning promotion West Ham reached the FA Cup final in 1923, the first to be played at Wembley Stadium.

The Hammers beat Norwich, Leeds, Huddersfield and Charlton in the early rounds. They then beat Sheffield United 1-0 at Old Trafford in front of 72,000 fans, a new record for an FA Cup semi-final.

On the day of the final against Bolton Wanderers at Wembley there were chaotic scenes. The game wasn't all-ticket which turned out to be a big mistake. Despite turnstiles being locked two hours before kickoff and crowds being told to turn back the gates were forced open.

It was estimated up to 300,000 were inside a stadium meant to hold 125,000. Many fans were on the pitch, leading to mounted police pushing them back. One grey horse named Billie clearly stood out on the black and white news footage. Despite his colour, the final became known as the 'White horse final' due to how he appeared on the images.

The game eventually kicked off 45 minutes late, with fans standing only just clear of the touchline. Bolton took the lead after two minutes and added a second in the 53rd minute. Afterwards Hammers trainer Charlie Paynter said players struggled to adapt to the pitch that was rutted by horse hooves.

FACT 18

1923
PROMOTION MAKES UP FOR CUP FINAL LOSS

A week after the disappointment of losing the FA Cup final, West Ham celebrated promotion to Division One.

The 1922-23 season started badly for the Hammers and they won just three of their first fifteen games. However they then lost just once between 11th November and the end of the season.

West Ham were locked in a three way battle with Leicester and Notts County for two promotion places. Two days after losing the cup final, the Hammers won 2-0 at Sheffield Wednesday to go top of the table on goal average. They would go up if they gained a point in their final game against Notts County on 5th May.

A crowd of 26,000 turned out at Upton Park for the crunch clash. At half-time things weren't good for West Ham as they trailed 1-0. However in the second half Leicester, who had been drawing at the interval of their game against Bury, conceded twice.

As news came through of Leicester's defeat, an almighty roar went around the ground. Play even stopped briefly while County's centre half gave and Hammers captain George Kay shook hands. Both sides were now sure of promotion and for the Hammers this more than made up for the cup final disappointment.

FACT 19

1925
VIC WATSON'S SCORING RECORD

In 1924-25 Vic Watson scored in ten consecutive league games for the Hammers, a club record that has not been equalled since.

Watson began his sequence with two goals in a 4-1 win over Sunderland on 20th December 1924. He then got one in a 3-2 victory against Cardiff on Christmas Day, but although he was also on the scoresheet against the same opposition the next day, the Hammers lost 2-1.

The Hammers were back in action for the third day running on 27th December, losing 3-2 at Preston, with Watson scoring once. They returned to winning ways in the New Year, with Watson scoring in a 2-0 home win over Blackburn. He was also on target in a 2-1 victory at Huddersfield and 2-0 win over Aston Villa at Upton Park.

Watson scored for the eighth game in succession on 7th February, when the Hammers won 4-0 at home against Manchester City. The next two games were away at Bury and Burnley and both ended in defeats, but Watson was on target in each of them.

Watson, who joined the club from non-league Wellingborough five years earlier for just £50, finished the season as West Ham's top scorer with 22 goals as they finished thirteenth in the league.

1927
SEVEN GOAL THRASHING

FACT 20

A West Ham side that had title aspirations were thrashed 7-0 at Everton on 22nd October 1927.

The Hammers were fourth in the table but were just a point off the top and had a game in hand on all three sides above them. Everton were one of those, ahead on goal average.

Two West Ham players, Stan Earle and Ted Hufton, were on international duty, but Everton were also missing their star striker Dixie Dean.

The home side were 2-0 up after 22 minutes as West Ham's defence struggled to cope with fast attacking play which made good use of the wingers. Any hopes of a comeback were dashed soon after half-time when Billy Henderson turned the ball into his own net.

Nothing could be done about Everton's fourth and fifth goals, which both came from sublime skill. The sixth however was from a penalty after a foul by Jim Barrett. Everton's reserve centre forward Tommy White, standing in for Dean, completed the scoring in the last minute.

The result showed how the Hammers still had much to learn to become a major force and that season Everton finished as champions. It is one of three games that share the record for West Ham's record defeat, the others being against Barnsley in 1919 and Sheffield Wednesday in 1959.

FACT 21

1929
A SECOND HALF DOUBLE HAT-TRICK

When West Ham thrashed Leeds 8-2 on 9th February 1929, Vic Watson got six of the goals, all of them coming in the second half.

Going into this fixture the Hammers were only just above the relegation zone and Leeds were challenging near the top of table. The first half was a tight affair with the Hammers taking a 2-0 lead through Vivian Gibbins and Tommy Yews, only for Leeds to draw level before the break.

In the second half though Watson took total control. The game was played on a heavy pitch but he was a strong man with a hard shot who had no problem adapting to the conditions. Time and time again Watson received a long ball, played it out to Yews on the wing and positioned himself in the box for the cross. The Leeds defence, who were an unfamiliar pairing, and their reserve keeper had no answer to Watson's brilliance.

This was West Ham's biggest win in a season where they scored 86 goals but conceded 96. Watson got 42 of the goals and today remains the all time club record scorer, totalling 326 in his fifteen years with the club (1920-35).

FACT 22

1931
A POSTHUMOUS TESTIMONIAL

The only time the Hammers have held a testimonial game for a player after their death was in 1931 for former centre half Frank Piercy.

Born in 1880, Piercy played in the first game at Upton Park in 1904 and was appointed captain in 1907. He was the first player to clock up 200 games for West Ham and on retiring from playing in 1912, he became an assistant trainer. He was a good all round sportsman who played cricket and had a golf handicap of just two.

Piercy died in June 1931. What was thought to be an ear problem was actually meningitis and he slipped into a coma. As a loyal servant to the club, a testimonial was granted with all proceeds going to his widow and three children.

On 1st October the Hammers faced an Isthmian League XI at Upton Park. A strong lineup defeated the amateurs 5-0 in front of what was described in the next match programme as a 'good number'. It reported that they hoped to hand a substantial sum to his widow.

FACT 23

1932
RELEGATED

The Hammers were relegated in 1931-32 after a terrible run of form in their last ten games.

They began the season brightly with wins in their opening two games, but they soon fell off the pace and were in the bottom two by the middle of October. They then rallied and were sixteenth by the end of the year.

Results continued to be mixed in the New Year but when West Ham beat Derby County 2-1 at Upton Park on 12th March there was no great cause for concern. The result left them comfortably placed in fourteenth position.

West Ham lost their next two games before picking up a well earned point against Arsenal. They then lost successive games 6-1 and 7-2 to set alarm bells ringing. Three more defeats followed, including a 6-1 mauling at Everton.

In their penultimate game, the Hammers lost 2-0 at Sunderland to fall into the bottom two. They now needed to win their final game at Chelsea and hope Blackpool lost at Sheffield United. The Hammers went down 3-2 at Stamford Bridge meaning they were back in Division Two after nine years in the top flight.

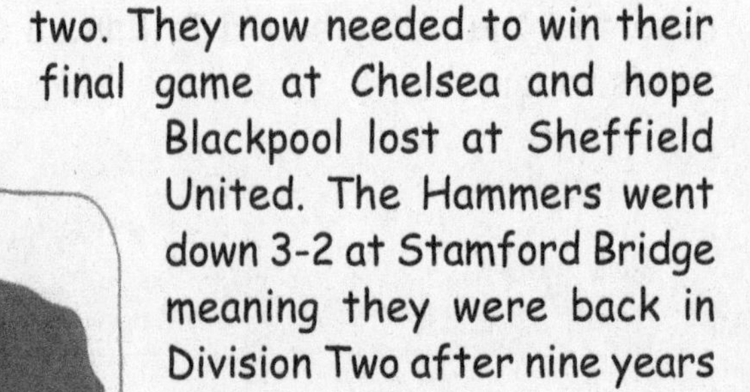

FACT 24

1932
SYD KING LEAVES

After thirty years in charge Syd King, at the time the only manager the club had ever had, left in 1932.

King had joined Thames Ironworks as a player in 1899 and remained when West Ham were formed. He continued playing for three more years, the last of which were combined with the role of secretary which was effectively the team manager position.

During King's time as manager he took the club from the Southern League up to Division One and the FA Cup final. He was a larger than life character with a captivating personality. He had short grey hair and flowing moustache and whilst in his office he would often send players to the Boleyn pub so they could bring him back bottles of beer.

West Ham remained in the top flight for nine years after promotion in 1923. However they had a poor start to the 1932-33 season and King was dismissed and succeeded by Charlie Paynter in November.

King's reputation for drinking and unconfirmed accusations that he had been stealing club funds meant he had no chance of securing another job in football. The following year, after having suffered a mental breakdown, he committed suicide by drinking alcohol mixed with corrosive liquid.

1933
PACIFIC COMBINATION

FACT **25**

On 16th October 1933 West Ham played a friendly match at Upton Park against a combined Peru-Chile XI.

The South American tourists, who billed themselves as the Combinado de Pacifico (Pacific Combination), were on a mammoth six month tour of Europe. The match against the Hammers was their sixth of the tour and they were unbeaten so far, having had impressive wins over Celtic and Newcastle.

Although dubbed as a Peru-Chile XI, the vast majority of the opposition squad were from Peru. Six of them had played in the 1930 World Cup and thirteen players alone came from the Universitario club.

Prior to kick off the South American players presented small red and white flags to their West Ham counterparts. The game was a hard but cleanly fought one and ended up in a 2-2 draw. Vic Watson and Jimmy Woods scored for the Hammers against a side whose players showed some great individual skills, but also communicated well with each other.

The tourists remained in Europe until the following February, going on to play games in Holland, France, Germany, Czechoslovakia and Italy.

FACT 26

1939 EXPUNGED GAMES

The outbreak of World War Two in September 1939 led to the immediate suspension of the Football League, meaning three West Ham United games were expunged from the record books.

War already looked inevitable when West Ham opened the 1939-40 season with a 3-1 win at Plymouth on 26th August. Two days later they beat Fulham 2-1 at Upton Park. All the goals came in the first half and Ted Fenton and Jackie Wood were on target for the Hammers.

The following day Wood, along with Harry Medhurst and Archie Macauley, reported to their territorial army units having been called up to man anti-aircraft guns.

On Friday 1st September Germany invaded Poland, a country which Britain had committed to defending if attacked. The game against Leicester went ahead at Upton Park the next day, with the visitors winning 2-0 thanks to two second half goals. It was then no surprise on the Sunday that Prime Minister Neville Chamberlain announced that Britain had declared war on Germany.

On 6th September the Football League announced the cancellation of that season's competition and three weeks later regional competitions were organised. All games played at the beginning of 1939-40 were then wiped from official records.

FACT 27

1940 THE FOOTBALL LEAGUE WAR CUP

The first club captain to lift a trophy at Wembley was Charlie Bicknell, who climbed the steps to receive the Football League War Cup in 1940.

The competition ran along similar lines to the FA Cup and was condensed into a seven week period that began at the end of April 1940. The Hammers beat Chelsea, Leicester, Huddersfield and Birmingham to reach the semi-final. This was played against Fulham at Stamford Bridge and the Hammers stormed into a 4-0 lead but were left holding on at the end as they were pegged back to 4-3.

Blackburn Rovers were the opponents at Wembley. In front of 42,339 fans Sam Small scored for the Hammers in the 34th minute, being first to the ball after the keeper had parried a George Foreman shot.

The game was end to end and both sides had opportunities to score. Blackburn were the better side in the closing stages as West Ham tired, but they defended well to hold on to their lead.

After being presented with the cup the players did a quick lap of honour but there were no great celebrations. Several players had to return to their army units, while some others returned to Upton Park for a few drinks in the Boleyn pub.

FACT 28

1944 UPTON PARK BOMBED

United's Upton Park ground was bombed during World War Two, meaning they had to play away from home for four months.

The V-1 flying bomb dropped by the German Luftwaffe in August 1944 landed between the line of the penalty area and touchline. It left a large crater and although nobody was killed it destroyed a large part of the South Bank Terrace. There was also damage to some of the Main Stand, including one dressing room. The resulting fire gutted the club offices and destroyed many of the documents and archives.

Due to the extent of the damage, which cost the club several thousand pounds, the Hammers had to play their next fourteen games away from home. The inconvenience didn't have any great impact on the team as they managed to win nine games in a row. When they returned to Upton Park in December, they lost their first game back there, 1-0 at home to Tottenham.

Upton Park was not the only London ground to suffer bomb damage during the war. Arsenal, Clapton Orient, Fulham and Millwall were also affected.

1946
A FOUR GOAL DEBUT

FACT 29

Don Travis scored four goals on his West Ham debut in the Wartime League but he failed to build on his great start.

Travis joined the Hammers from the merchant navy and made his debut on 16th February 1946 against Plymouth at Upton Park. The 22 year old centre forward was tall, strong and quick to seize on opportunities, to the delight of the 17,000 crowd.

On a muddy pitch, Archie Macauley twice set up Travis to score in the first half. Early in the second half he completed a hat-trick with a fine individual goal, using his strength to power through the opposition defence and score with his left foot.

Terry Woodgate then hit a hat-trick of his own within an eight minute spell. Before the end Macauley got his third assist of the afternoon, setting up Travis for his fourth goal to make it 7-0. Plymouth's misery was completed when they missed a penalty.

Travis had hit four goals on his first team debut just as he had done for the reserves. However when organised competition resumed he failed to find the same form. He played just five times over two seasons without scoring, before being sold to Southend.

FACT 30

1948
AN IMPORTANT APPOINTMENT

In 1948 the West Ham board made an appointment that would lay the foundations for future success.

With manager Charlie Paynter now in his late sixties, he asked the board to approach former Hammers wing half Ted Fenton about becoming his assistant. Fenton had joined Southern League Colchester as player-manager two years earlier and taken them to the fifth round of the FA Cup.

Fenton came to Upton Park specifically to learn the ropes from Paynter until he was ready to retire. This took place in the summer of 1950, although he retained an affiliation with the club as a special ambassador.

Whilst manager at West Ham, Fenton developed a youth policy that would see the development of the likes of Bobby Moore and Geoff Hurst. The club reached the FA Youth Cup final three times in four years in the late 1950s. He also encouraged players to take coaching badges so they were ready for when they stopped playing.

In 1958 Fenton gained promotion to Division One and finished sixth in his first season. However in 1961 he was replaced by Ron Greenwood in circumstances that were never fully explained.

FACT 31

1950
CHARLIE PAYNTER RETIRES

In 1950 one club man Charlie Paynter retired as manager, bringing an end to a fifty year association with the Hammers.

Paynter was born in Swindon in 1879 but spent his childhood in Plaistow, playing youth football. He joined Thames Ironworks as a volunteer helper in 1897 and stayed when West Ham United were formed.

After sustaining an injury whilst playing for the reserves, Paynter became Syd King's trainer in 1902. He was an ideal link between the players and manager and was also able to use his knowledge of physiotherapy to treat injuries. His experience led to him being called upon to help with the England side on occasions too.

When King was sacked in 1932, Paynter took over but he wasn't able to take the Hammers back up to Division One. He moulded a good side that was consistently in the top half of the table but the outbreak of World War Two caused this to break up.

Paynter's retirement meant that the Hammers would now appoint only their third manager in fifty years. However there was no need for a search as the board had already agreed two years earlier that Ted Fenton would succeed him.

FACT 32

1954
ABANDONMENT AT 4-1

West Ham were desperately unlucky on 2nd January 1954 when their game with Stoke was abandoned with just six minutes remaining as they led 4-1.

The Hammers led 3-0 at half-time but during the second period a thick fog descended. Even though only six minutes remained, visibility was so bad that the referee had no option but to end the game.

League rules stipulated that in the case of an abandoned game the whole ninety minutes had to replayed. This meant the teams faced each other again on 12th April which was a Monday afternoon.

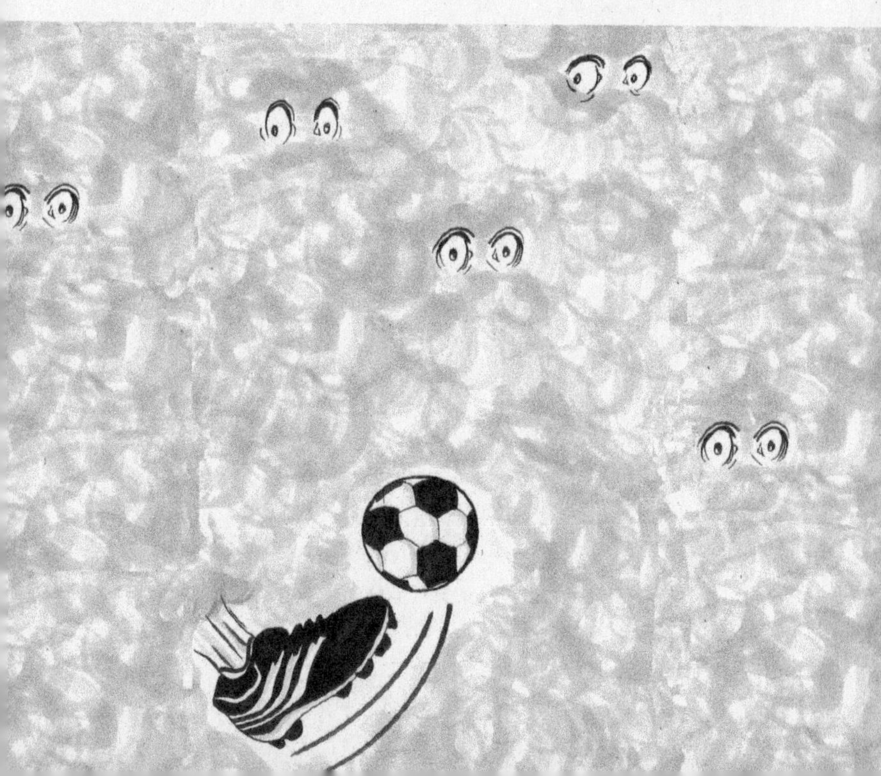

The game attracted the lowest home attendance of the season, just 10,449.

The match ended 2-2 although had the original result even been allowed to stand it would have made no difference to their final league position. The Hammers finished in thirteenth, two points behind Doncaster in the days of only two points for a win. Stoke City, however would have fallen from eleventh to twelfth had the first result stood, remaining above the Hammers on goal average.

1954
FLOODLIT FRIENDLIES

FACT 33

In the autumn of 1954 some of the biggest names in European football came to Upton Park as West Ham hosted a series of prestige floodlit friendlies.

The lights had been installed the previous year but they weren't allowed to be used for Football League and FA Cup matches. With the Hammers struggling in Division Two, these games were arranged to give the fans some extra interest and generate extra revenue as promotion wasn't looking likely.

The first big friendly was against Stuttgart who were beaten 4-0. The Hammers then had a comfortable 3-1 victory over Austrian side WAC. Both these games had been in October, but the Hammers were in for a shock when they faced Italian giants AC Milan on 14th December.

The Milan side included Juan Schiaffino, the most expensive player in the world at the time, as well as two players who had represented Italy in that year's World Cup.

Milan were just too good for the home side, who wore white to avoid a colour clash with the opposition's red and black striped shirts. Watched by a crowd of 35,000, the Hammers were 2-0 down at half-time and four goals in the last half hour meant the game ended 6-0. The crowd were gallant in defeat though, applauding the Italians off at the end.

FACT 34

1955 RECORD LOW HOME ATTENDANCE

The lowest home crowd was on 12th February 1955 when less than 5,000 fans attended a Division Two game at Upton Park.

The Hammers hadn't lost at home in the league since August but various factors led to just 4,373 turning out to see this home defeat by Doncaster. It was a Thursday afternoon so many fans were in work or school, it was unattractive opposition and it was also a freezing old day.

On a snow covered pitch West Ham had most of the play in the first half without finding the net. Shortly before the hour mark some poor positioning by Hammers' keeper George Taylor gifted a goal to Doncaster forward Jimmy Walker.

With very little crowd to back them, the Hammers were unable to raise their game and were more likely to go further behind than equalise.

In the next home game at home to Leeds normal service was resumed on and off the pitch. 19,664 turned out to see the Hammers beat Leeds 2-1 in a season where they finished eighth in the table.

FACT 35

1955
WINNING ON HIS WEDDING DAY

On the afternoon of 5th March 1955 Harry Hooper got married before captaining the Hammers to victory over Leeds.

The 21 year old winger married Margaret Austin at Emmanuel Church in Forest Gate before heading to Upton Park, where he was made captain for the day. Les Bennett and Albert Foan scored for the Hammers as they beat Leeds 2-1 in front of a crowd of 19,694. Hooper had a hand in Bennett's goal, which came from the rebound after his shot had been headed off the line.

After the game Hooper was toasted with champagne in the dressing room and he then returned to his new wife and the wedding reception which took place in Ilford. The couple had a brief honeymoon in Sussex and announced they would be going to Spain at the end of the season.

Hooper had not been the first Hammers player to get married and play a game. Two years earlier right back George Wright did the same thing but he was not so lucky in the game, with Doncaster winning 3-1.

FACT 36

1957
CAREER CUT SHORT BY TUBERCULOSIS

Defender Malcolm Allison had to stop playing soon after his thirtieth birthday after he contracted tuberculosis.

Allison was a reliable central defender who made over 250 appearances in all competitions during a six year spell with the club. However he fell ill in September 1957 and collapsed whilst walking down some stairs at Upton Park. Prior to an away match at Sheffield United he was up coughing all night and although he played in the game, it turned out to be his last appearance.

Allison didn't drink or smoke and was mystified by his ill health, but tuberculosis was diagnosed. This led to doctors operating and removing part of his left lung. Although he tried his hardest and turned out for the reserves, he was unable to get fit enough to play professionally again.

After a brief spell in the non-league with Romford, Allison turned to coaching youngsters at West Ham, including future captain Bobby Moore. He got his first crack at management with Bath City in 1963 and went on to enjoy a long and varied career both in England and abroad.

FACT 37

1958
PROMOTED WITH RECORD GOALS HAUL

West Ham finally returned to Division One in 1958 when they won promotion and scored 101 goals, still a club record.

The Hammers didn't get off to a good start, winning only three of their first ten games. However in October they found their form, winning six from the next seven and netting five goals in two of those games.

On 18th January 1958 a 6-2 home win over Swansea took the Hammers to the top of the table. This was the third time in just six games that they had scored six. On 8th March they went even better, hammering Doncaster 8-0 at Upton Park.

After that Swansea victory West Ham remained top of the table, save for one week in February, for the rest of the campaign. However they could not shake off the challenge of Charlton, Blackburn and Liverpool. A 1-1 home draw with Liverpool in their penultimate game meant promotion was almost certain due to their superior goal average, but the Hammers could still be denied by a freak set of results on the last day.

On 26th April 1958 the Hammers made no mistake and won 3-1 against Middlesbrough at Ayresome Park, passing the 100 goal mark. The top league scorer was John Dick with 21 and they went up as champions.

FACT 38

1958
CHRISTMAS DAY

Up until sixty years ago it was commonplace for Football League fixtures to take place on Christmas Day. West Ham played 47 times in all competitions on 25th December, the last occasion being in 1958.

The Hammers had settled back into Division One quite well and were tenth in the table when struggling Tottenham Hotspur came to Upton Park for a derby fixture.

The match kicked off at 11am, allowing fans time to get back to their families for their Christmas dinner. The match programme contained a message from the directors extending 'their heartiest seasons greetings to all their friends in the realm of soccer both at home and away.' The attendance was 26,178 which was higher than average, but considerably lower than when Arsenal and Chelsea had visited Upton Park earlier in the season.

Goals from Vic Keble and John Dick gave the Hammers a 2-1 victory. The following day the two sides met at White Hart Lane and West Ham triumphed again, winning 4-1 with Dick and Keble again getting on the scoresheet.

FACT 39

1960
GEOFF HURST

In February 1960 Geoff Hurst made an underwhelming start to his West Ham career, as he wasn't sure whether to concentrate on football or cricket in the long term.

Hurst joined the Hammers as an apprentice in 1958 and signed professional forms the following year. Injuries to the squad meant he made his debut aged eighteen years and two months on 27th February 1960 in a 3-1 defeat away to Nottingham Forest.

By his own admission Hurst had an indifferent debut and played only twice more that season. In 1960-61 he played just six times and considered giving up football to concentrate on cricket for Essex.

Ron Greenwood's appointment as manager in April 1961 was a boost for Hurst. More emphasis was now put on football skill than physical strength. In Greenwood's first season Hurst played 24 times in a left midfield position.

Hurst was moved to centre forward for 1962-63 and scored thirteen goals in 27 games. Having played just one county championship game for Essex in 1962, Hurst finally gave up cricket two years later after winning the FA Cup with the Hammers.

Hurst became a legend with the Hammers and also England, scoring a hat-trick in the World Cup final in 1966. When he left the club in 1972, he had scored 242 goals in 500 appearances.

FACT 40

1960
SHOOTING DOWN THE GUNNERS

West Ham gave their London rivals Arsenal a footballing lesson on 5th November 1960, thrashing the team nicknamed the Gunners 6-0 at Upton Park.

The Hammers were in tenth place, three points behind Arsenal who were in eighth. However it took just three minutes for the home side to take the lead, Dave Dunmore seizing upon a poor clearance to score. Dunmore added a second soon after the half hour, scoring with a great shot after receiving a pass from Phil Woosnam.

After 71 minutes John Dick scored the third after Arsenal's defence failed to properly clear a ball that had become stuck in the mud. Woosnam made it 4-0 seven minutes later, firing into the roof of the net after the keeper had beaten out two other efforts.

A great strike from Andy Malcolm, his first goal in three years, gave the Hammers a 5-0 lead with six minutes left. Dunmore completed the rout and his hat-trick with a minute to go, scoring with a low shot that the keeper could only help into the goal.

Dunmore may have got a hat-trick, but special praise was reserved by the press for Woosnam as he scored one and created four others. West Ham's dominance was emphasised by the fact that keeper Jack Kelsey was Arsenal's best player.

FACT 41

1961
RON GREENWOOD

The first managerial appointment who had no previous connection to the club was Ron Greenwood in 1961.

A former player with Brentford, Chelsea and Fulham, Greenwood was an assistant manager at Arsenal when Ted Fenton was sacked in March 1961. The club never fully explained the reasons for his dismissal, saying it was a behind the scenes matter.

Greenwood took over the following month and continued to nurture the talent that had been developed by Fenton. He didn't overcomplicate matters with detailed tactics, instead allowing players to use their individual skills to win games. His methods led West Ham to their first major trophy in 1964 then a European triumph the following year.

In 1974 Greenwood became the general manager with John Lyall in charge of team affairs. His association with the Hammers came to an end in 1977 when he succeeded Don Revie as manager of England.

Greenwood died in 2006 from Alzheimer's disease in Suffolk. The following year a blue plaque was unveiled by the Heritage Foundation in his honour at Upton Park.

FACT 42

1962
RECORD TOP FLIGHT AWAY WIN

The club's biggest away win away in the top flight was on 8th September 1962 when they thrashed Manchester City 6-1 at Maine Road.

It was a masterful performance by Ron Greenwood's side of precision passing which rarely gave the opposition a glimpse of the ball. Malcolm Musgrove scored the opening goal after 26 minutes and although Young equalised two minutes later, it only led to the Hammers taking total control.

In a devastating ten minute spell before half-time Tony Scott, Johnny Byrne and Martin Peters scored to give West Ham a commanding 4-1 lead. With twenty minutes remaining Musgrove headed his second, after which City keeper Bert Trautmann was sent off for kicking the ball at referee Ken Stokes.

Despite City being down to ten men with outfield player Alan Oakes in goal, the Hammers could only add one more to their tally. With ten minutes left Geoff Hurst slotted home after good work by Byrne on the left, to make it 6-1. Coincidentally, West Ham beat City by the same scoreline at Upton Park later in the season.

FACT 43 — 1963 INTERNATIONAL SOCCER LEAGUE

Rather than have the summer off in 1963, West Ham crossed the Atlantic Ocean to take part in the International Soccer League.

The summer tournament began at the end of May with games being played across the United States. The Hammers started slowly, drawing with Kilmarnock then losing to Italians Mantova. They were then boosted by the arrival of Bobby Moore and Johnny Byrne, who had been on England duty, and won three in succession.

The last game against Brazilians Recife kicked off at midnight due to the extreme heat in New York. The Hammers drew 1-1 leaving them top of their section. They had been away for over four weeks and went home for a month, then returned at the end of July for the two legged final against Polish side Gornik Zabrze.

Both games were played at Randall's Island, New York. The first ended 1-1 and in the second Geoff Hurst scored the only goal to win the ISL Playoff Trophy. This meant qualification for the prestigious American Challenge Cup final, but the Hammers lost 2-1 on aggregate to Dukla Prague.

Despite the lengthy summer, it had no detrimental impact on the squad as the next few seasons would be some of the most memorable in the club's history.

FACT 44

1964 FA CUP FINAL COMEBACK

The Hammers won their first major trophy in 1964, twice coming from behind to beat Preston with a dramatic late winner in the FA Cup final.

The Hammers fell behind to their Division Two opponents after just ten minutes when Jim Standen spilled the ball into the path of Doug Holden who bundled it over the line. They were soon level though when teenager John Sissons equalised with a low shot. Shortly before half-time Preston went ahead again, Ally Dawson's powerful header giving Standen no chance.

Seven minutes into the second half West Ham were level when Geoff Hurst's header hit the underside of the bar and bounced into the net off Preston's keeper Alan Kelly.

Both sets of players tired as the game wore on and it looked like extra time would be necessary. Then with a minute remaining Hurst played the ball out to Bradbrooke on the right. He crossed for Ronnie Boyce to head the ball out of the keeper's reach into the corner of the net.

There was no way back for Preston now and Bobby Moore climbed the steps to receive the trophy from Lord Harwood. The victory showed how the youth development policy of the 1950s had paid off, with eight of the team having come through the junior ranks.

FACT 45

1965
EUROPEAN GLORY

West Ham's first season in European competition ended in glory as they triumphed in the final of the European Cup Winners Cup at Wembley.

The Hammers reached the final with victories over La Gantoise, Sparta Prague, Lausanne and Real Zaragoza. Their opponents on 19th May were Germans 1860 Munich, whose supporters were vastly outnumbered in the crowd of over 97,000.

Both sides produced open attractive football. The Hammers had the best chances in a first half in which John Sissons fell over with the goal gaping. Geoff Hurst also had a magnificent shot from outside the area well saved and it remained 0-0 at the break.

The deadlock was broken in the seventieth minute when Alan Sealey collected a pass from Ronnie Boyce who had won a tackle in midfield. He controlled the ball well then beat the keeper from a difficult angle, firing the ball into the top corner of the net. Two minutes after opening the scoring Sealey was on target again, beating the keeper after Martin Peters had nodded down a Bobby Moore free kick.

There was no further scoring and Moore climbed the Wembley steps afterwards to collect the cup. The Hammers had become only the second English side to win a European trophy.

FACT **46**

1965 FIVE GOALS IN TWENTY MINUTES

Striker Brian Dear was in sensational form on 16th April 1965, scoring five goals in record time.

Dear came through the youth system and made his debut in 1962-63, but didn't get a consistent run in the side until March 1965.

In a league game against West Bromwich Albion, Dear's first goal came after 44 minutes and was a simple tap in. He then scored four in the first nineteen minutes of the second half of a match the Hammers won 6-1.

Dear had set a new record for the time scoring five goals, which he still lays claim to today.

Sergio

Aguero was also credited with five in twenty minutes for Manchester City against Newcastle in 2015. However Dear points to the fact there was no first half injury time in his match, compared to three in Aguero's.

Dear's final tally that season was an impressive fourteen goals in fifteen games in all competitions. However the presence of Geoff Hurst, Martin Peters, and Johnny Byrne meant his appearances were limited. In seven years at Upton Park, Dear scored 33 goals in league 65 appearances before leaving for Fulham in 1969.

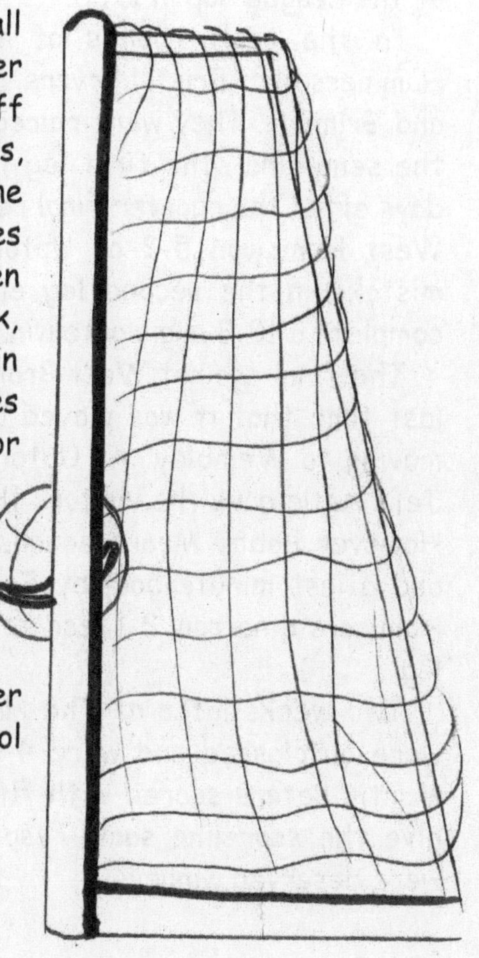

Dear re-joined the Hammers the following year, but never played for the club again after the Blackpool incident of 1971.

FACT 47

1966 LEAGUE CUP FINALISTS

West Ham missed out on winning a trophy for the third season running when they were beaten finalists of the League Cup in 1966.

In the early rounds of the competition the Hammers beat Bristol Rovers, Mansfield, Rotherham and Grimsby. They were paired with Cardiff City in the semi-final, the first leg taking place just five days after the quarter-final replay against Grimsby. West Ham won 5-2 at Upton Park and made no mistake in the second leg either, winning 5-1 to complete a 10-3 aggregate win.

The final against West Bromwich Albion was the last time that it was played over two legs before moving to Wembley. At Upton Park on 9th March, Jeff Astle gave the visitors the lead after an hour. However Bobby Moore equalised from forty yards and a last minute goal by Johnny Byrne gave the Hammers a narrow 2-1 lead to take into the second leg.

Two weeks later at The Hawthorns, West Ham were outclassed and were 4-0 down at half-time. Martin Peters scored with fifteen minutes left to give the scoreline some respectability but Albion were deserved winners.

FACT 48 — 1966 WORLD CUP WINNERS

The club made a huge contribution to England's World Cup win in 1966.

Three Hammers players were involved in the tournament; Geoff Hurst, Bobby Moore, who was also captain, and Martin Peters.

In the quarter-final at Wembley Hurst scored the only goal of the game against Argentina. The semi-final saw England beat Portugal 2-1, with Hurst setting up the second goal for Bobby Charlton.

In the final West Germany led early on only for England to come back and lead 2-1 thanks to goals from Peters and Hurst. A late equaliser forced extra time in which Hurst scored two of the most famous goals ever scored at Wembley. He made it 3-2 with a hotly contested goal, given by the linesman who adjudged it to have bounced over the line after hitting the crossbar.

The goal that completed Hurst's hat-trick was in the last moments, when he broke clear and scored as commentator Kenneth Wolstenholme uttered the famous phrase 'Some people are on the pitch, they think its all over, it is now.'

Moore collected the World Cup from the Queen. One of the first photographs was of him with the cup sat on the shoulders of Hurst and Ray Wilson, with Peters stood beside them. This scene was depicted in a statue unveiled near Upton Park in 2003.

FACT 49 — 1967 LONDON FIVE-A-SIDE CHAMPIONS

West Ham triumphed at Wembley for a third and what is now largely forgotten time in 1967, when they were crowned London's five a side champions.

The Hammers had been regular participants in the post season competition that was inaugurated at the Empire Pool in Wembley in 1954.

All the games were played on the one evening, 10th May 1967 in front of a capacity crowd of 8,500. The tournament was endorsed by the Football Association and covered in an ITV sports highlights programme.

The Hammers were given a bye in the first round then Geoff Hurst hit a hat-trick in a 3-0 win over QPR. Martin Peters and Bobby Moore then scored the goals as Charlton were beaten 2-1 in the semi-final.

The final was against Arsenal and a comfortable 4-0 win for the Hammers who were too fast for their opponents. Ron Boyce scored first and then Hurst got another hat-trick, one of the goals being a penalty.

West Ham had finally won the tournament, having been beaten finalists on three previous occasions. They triumphed twice more before the competition was disbanded in the early 1980s.

FACT 50

1967
TREVOR BROOKING

A teenager who would play a major part in West Ham's history over the next fifty years made his debut on 29th August 1967.

Trevor Brooking was still a month away from his nineteenth birthday when he made his debut at outside right in a 3-3 draw at Burnley. He went on to make 28 appearances that season, scoring nine goals including a hat-trick in a 5-0 home win over Newcastle.

Playing mainly in midfield, Brooking won the FA Cup twice with the Hammers, scoring the winning goal in the 1980 final. He made a total of 647 career appearances, scoring 102 goals. He was also capped 47 times by England. A gentleman player, he was rarely booked and always respected the referee's decision.

Brooking played his last game for West Ham in 1984. Rather than head into management, he went into media punditry and football administration. He was a board member at Upton Park and twice stepped in as caretaker manager in 2003.

Already a MBE and CBE, Brooking was knighted for services to sport in 2004. In 2009 a stand was named after him at Upton Park and when the Hammers moved to the Olympic Stadium in 2016 one was named after him there as well.

FACT 51

1968
END OF THE CHICKEN RUN

The final home game of the 1967-68 season against Coventry City was the last time that fans could stand on the terrace that had become known as the 'Chicken Run'.

The terrace had got its name due to it being constructed of wood and surrounded by wire mesh. It was intimidating for the opposition players due to it being within touching distance of the pitch. However, the terrace was hardly fit for purpose, primitive in appearance and with a huge accumulation of litter underneath the timber bleachers.

The cover of the match programme against Coventry City on 4th May 1968 contained a photograph of the terrace. The editorial regretted fans would have to stand elsewhere while a new stand was being constructed, but hoped to see them back there eventually.

Two days after the Hammers had drawn 0-0 with Coventry, the bulldozers moved in. Early in 1969, a new paddock with a 3,500 seat stand behind it was completed.

Although the new standing area was officially named the East Terrace, fans generally referred to it as the Chicken Run until it was seated in the 1990s.

FACT 52

1968
HURST SCORES SIX IN RECORD TOP FLIGHT WIN

West Ham's biggest top flight victory is an 8-0 win over Sunderland at Upton Park on 19th October 1968, a game in which Geoff Hurst scored six goals.

It took nineteen minutes for the Hammers to open the scoring, Martin Peters crossing for Hurst to score a goal he would later admit had gone in off his hand. Bobby Moore made it 2-0 with a free kick then Hurst got his second with a close range header. On the stroke of half-time he completed his first hat-trick, scoring from Harry Redknapp's corner.

Hurst got his fourth with a fierce shot after a brilliant knock down by Martin Peters, then bundled the ball over the line for his fifth. Trevor Brooking made it 7-0 with a great effort from outside the area before Hurst was set up by Redknapp to complete his double hat-trick.

Later in the season the Hammers lost the return fixture 2-1 at Roker Park. In 2013, following an appeal by Hurst himself, film footage of the game came to light which is accompanied by the crowd noise but no commentary.

FACT 53

1969 COLOUR MATCH OF THE DAY

The Hammers made British television football history on 15th November 1969 when they featured in the first colour transmission of the BBC's iconic *Match of the Day* highlights programme.

The BBC had been phasing in colour broadcasts over the last few years, but 15th November 1969 was the date set for it to extend to all programmes, not just selected ones. As well as *Match of the Day*, other programmes being shown that day included the *Harry Secombe Show* and *Dixon of Dock Green.*

For the first colour football broadcast, West Ham's away game at Liverpool was a perfect choice. Anfield wasa noisy and colourful venue, both teams wore bright strips, while West Ham's side contained a number of well known players.

There was no joy for the Hammers who lost the game 2-0. That evening, starting at five past ten, 35 minutes of the game were shown on BBC1. The programme was presented by David Coleman and watched by up to ten million viewers. Television coverage of football had been changed forever and West Ham were part of it.

1970
RECORD ATTENDANCE

FACT 54

The record confirmed attendance for a match at Upton Park was on 17th October 1970 when 42,322 fans attended a league game between against Tottenham Hotspur.

The Hammers had endured a bad start to 1970-71 and didn't register a win until their eleventh game against Burnley. The following week, a record crowd crammed into Upton Park, where Alan Mullery gave Spurs a sixth minute lead. Midway through the first half Peter Eustace equalised with a header from Bobby Moore's free kick.

Eight minutes before half-time Mike England headed Spurs back into the lead. However early in the second half he gifted West Ham an equaliser when his poor backpass was intercepted by Geoff Hurst who steered the ball into the net.

Whether the crowd of 42,322 was Upton Park's record attendance remains open to debate. Tottenham's record books list two occasions prior to World War Two when slightly higher crowds watched fixtures between the two teams. However as West Ham records were lost during the air raid of 1944, the club maintain any crowds from that period were estimates and continue to refer to the 1970 game as an attendance record.

FACT 55

1971 BLACKPOOL ILLUMINATIONS

When West Ham were well beaten in an FA Cup game at Blackpool in 1971 it emerged four players had been drinking in a nightclub just twelve hours earlier.

The Hammers lost the third round tie 4-0, with one local news reporter describing their performance as 'utter humiliation and abject surrender'.

The following Monday morning the reason for the defeat became apparent. A fan reported to the club that he had seen Bobby Moore, Jimmy Greaves, Clyde Best and Brian Dear drinking in the 007 nightclub until the early hours. It transpired that they had gone there at the invitation of a BBC journalist and also been accompanied by the club physiotherapist.

All four players were fined one week's wages. As the senior professionals, Moore and Greaves were not named in the team until 9th February, and Dear never played for the Hammers again. Best was just a teenager at the time and did play the week after the incident.

Writing in his autobiography, Jimmy Greaves acknowledged that they had acted irresponsibly, but stated that they had expected the game to be postponed due to the icy conditions.

FACT 56

1972
THE FOUR GAME SEMI-FINAL

The Hammers were involved in an extraordinary League Cup semi-final with Stoke City in 1972 which was only settled after two replays.

In the first leg at the Victoria Ground in Stoke, a Geoff Hurst penalty and goal from Clyde Best gave the Hammers a 2-1 win. However back at Upton Park Stoke levelled the tie in the 72nd minute then Hurst had a late penalty saved by Gordon Banks. With away goals not counting, a replay was needed at Hillsborough in Sheffield.

Banks was again in outstanding form as the sides drew 0-0 in the replay, meaning a fourth game was required at Old Trafford, 49 days after the first leg. Bobby Moore was forced to go in goal for twenty minutes in the first half as keeper Bobby Ferguson received treatment. Even though he saved a penalty, he couldn't stop the rebound.

Despite the setback, West Ham fought back and went ahead thanks to goals from Billy Bonds and Trevor Brooking, only for Peter Dobing to equalise for Stoke before half-time. Four minutes after the interval Terry Conroy scored for Stoke and the Hammers couldn't find a way back. Finally, after seven hours of football the tie was over and Stoke went on to beat Chelsea in the final.

FACT 57

1972 THE MIDWEEK AFTERNOON FA CUP REPLAY

In 1972 power shortages meant that West Ham had to play an FA Cup replay on a midweek afternoon.

After the Hammers drew 0-0 at non-league Hereford in a fourth round tie, the replay was scheduled for Monday 14th February. Due to emergency power saving regulations imposed by the government because of a miners' strike, the game kicked off at 2.15pm.

Despite the inconvenient time, more than 42,000 fans squeezed into the ground with an estimated 5,000 locked out. Many of those climbed on to the top of flats behind the North Bank and clung on for dear life to watch the game.

Those lucky enough to be inside saw some wasteful finishing by West Ham before Geoff Hurst opened the scoring two minutes before half-time. Seven minutes after the interval he added a second and with a quarter of an hour left he completed his hat-trick. Hereford's consolation came with six minutes remaining.

Two years later the sides were drawn to play each other again. Hereford, now a Football League club, came to Upton Park in the third round of the FA Cup. Power shortages again meant an early kick off, the usual 3pm time being brought forward to 1.45pm. The Hammers were held to a 1-1 draw at Upton Park then subjected to a giant killing act in the replay, losing 2-1.

FACT 58

1973 WATNEY CUP PENALTIES

West Ham's first penalty shootout was in the Watney Cup, a short-lived summer competition for the top scorers in each of the Football League's four divisions.

The competition was first played in 1970 and in 1973 the Hammers qualified as they had scored 67 goals the previous season. Only Leeds and Liverpool had scored more, but they weren't eligible to compete as they had qualified for European competition.

In the first round West Ham were drawn away to Bristol Rovers of Division Three, who had won the competition the previous year. In front of 20,000 fans Rovers took the lead after half an hour but seven minutes before half-time Ted McDougall equalised for the Hammers.

There were no further goals in the second half but there was no extra time and instead the game went straight to penalties. This was the first time the Hammers had been involved in a penalty shootout and the first kick taken by Bryan Robson was saved. However, due to the keeper having moved, the referee ordered it to be retaken but this time he missed.

The following nine kicks were all converted meaning Rovers won the shootout 5-4. Stoke City, whose side contained Geoff Hurst, went on to win the competition in what turned out to be its final year.

FACT 59

1974
BOBBY MOORE LEAVES

West Ham United and England's legendary centre half Bobby Moore left the club in March 1974.

Moore broke into the side in 1958-59 at the age of just seventeen, taking over in defence from Malcolm Allison whose career was ended by tuberculosis. Moore captained the Hammers to an FA Cup win in 1964 followed by the European Cup Winners Cup a year later. He then captured the hearts of the nation when he lifted the World Cup in 1966.

In total he played 644 games for West Ham, scoring 27 goals. He was the club's record appearance holder until he was surpassed by Billy Bonds. His career at Upton Park spanned sixteen seasons, during which he was named Football Writers Player of the Year, BBC Sports Personality of the Year and runner up in the Ballon D'Or.

Moore got injured in an FA Cup tie with Hereford in January 1974 and never appeared for the Hammers again. He was sold two months later to Fulham for £25,000. Today his legacy lives on with stands having been named after him at Upton Park and then the London Stadium, while the number six shirt has been retired in his honour.

FACT 60

1975
THE LAST ALL ENGLISH FA CUP WINNERS

West Ham won the FA Cup for a second time in 1975, with their line-up consisting entirely of English players.

With John Lyall now installed as team manager and Ron Greenwood in a director of football type role, the Hammers beat Southampton, Swindon, QPR, Arsenal and Ipswich to reach the final. In a strange twist of fate, the Hammers would face ex captain Bobby Moore against Fulham at Wembley on 3rd May.

The first half was a close affair with Fulham belying their Division Two status and Moore having an outstanding game. After an hour however Alan Taylor, a 21 year old signed from Rochdale earlier in the season, took control when he scored twice in five minutes for the Hammers.

Both of Taylor's goals came when he was first to the rebound after Fulham's keeper could only parry shots. The young striker was lucky to be playing at all. Earlier in the season he had been injured when Rochdale played their games in the competition, meaning he wasn't cup tied.

After the final whistle West Ham's new captain Billy Bonds collected the cup. His team mates all, of them English, followed him to collect their medals. No cup winning side since has contained only English players.

FACT 61

1976 BEATEN EUROPEAN FINALISTS

In 1975-76 West Ham failed to repeat their European Cup Winners Cup success of eleven years earlier, having to instead settle for being beaten finalists.

The Hammers beat Reipas Lahti of Finland then Ararat Yerevan from the Soviet Union in the early rounds. The quarter final saw them overcome Dutch side Den Haag on away goals then in the semi-final they overcame a 2-1 first leg deficit to beat Eintracht Frankfurt 3-1.

The final saw West Ham up against Belgian side Anderlecht in their own national stadium, Heysel. Pat Holland gave the Hammers the lead shortly before the half hour mark but just before half-time Frank Lampard's misplaced backpass allowed Rob Rensenbrink to equalise.

Lampard was forced to leave the field injured two minutes after the break and soon afterwards Francois Van Der Elst put Anderlecht ahead. Keith Robson equalised midway through the half but with seventeen minutes left Anderlecht were controversially awarded a penalty. This was converted by Rensenbrink but television replays later showed Holland had fairly won the ball.

West Ham attacked in search of an equaliser but with two minutes to go their hopes of a second European triumph were ended when Van Der Elst broke clear to score. The Hammers have not made it to a European final since.

FACT 62

1978
GOOD RUN TOO LATE TO AVOID DROP

Despite improving form towards the end of 1977-78, it was not good enough to stop West Ham being relegated.

The Hammers lost their first three games before finally picking up points in a 3-2 win at Newcastle. However one win in the next fourteen left them third bottom in early December. In January two wins and a draw from four games lifted them out of the relegation zone, but they were back there after four straight defeats in March.

At Easter the Hammers went on a great run of five wins in seven games, but survival was still out of their hands. In their last game West Ham were in seventeenth and faced Liverpool at home, but other teams had games in hand. Even if the Hammers won they would face a nervous wait to see if they could survive.

On 29th April 1978 Liverpool won 2-0 at Upton Park to leave the Hammers third bottom. There was a glimmer of hope as Wolves had two games to play and if they lost both, West Ham would finish above them on goal difference. It didn't happen though and after two decades the Hammers were back in Division Two. Despite going down, the board remained loyal to manager John Lyall, which proved to be a wise decision.

FACT 63

1980 SECOND TIER FA CUP WINNERS

West Ham won their third FA Cup in 1980 whilst still in Division Two, an achievement no club has managed since.

West Ham beat three Division One sides to reach the final, where Arsenal were the overwhelming favourites. The game started slowly with Arsenal happy to keep possession and frustrate the opposition players.

The Hammers scored with their first real attack in the thirteenth minute. Alan Devonshire crossed into the box and David Cross's shot was blocked but only into the path of Stuart Pearson. He fired the ball back to the danger area and Trevor Brooking flicked a header into the goal.

West Ham spent the majority of the game defending their lead, with Phil Parkes in fine form in goal. In the closing stages seventeen year old Paul Allen broke free and looked set to put the Hammers 2-0 up, only to be brought down from behind by Willie Young. A clear goalscoring opportunity had been denied but Young was only yellow carded.

Captain Billy Bonds collected the cup from the Duchess of Kent as 'I'm Forever Blowing Bubbles' rang around Wembley. Although a number of second tier sides have made it to the final since, none of them have managed to overcome their top flight opposition.

1980
BEHIND CLOSED DOORS

FACT **64**

West Ham were forced by UEFA to play a European tie in a virtually empty Upton Park in 1980.

The Hammers were drawn against Spanish cup holders Castilla in the first round of the Cup Winners Cup. In the first leg in Madrid, the Spaniards won 3-1 and around fifty West Ham fans were removed from the stadium by police due to crowd disturbances.

UEFA initially ordered the Hammers play the second leg at Sunderland, but after an appeal they instead decided that the game could go ahead at Upton Park, but with no fans allowed entry into the ground.

On 1st October 1980, there were just 262 spectators in the ground, all of them club officials and journalists. Despite the eerie atmosphere, the Hammers scored three times without reply in the first half to overturn the deficit.

In the 56th minute Bernal scored a spectacular goal from 35 yards to level the tie. There were no further goals in the second half, meaning extra time was needed. David Cross scored twice to complete his hat-trick and a 6-4 aggregate victory for the Hammers.

West Ham overcame Politehnica Timisoara in the next round but were beaten in the quarter-final by eventual winners Dinamo Tblisi.

FACT 65

1981 LEAGUE CUP FINALISTS

In the Hammers second League Cup final and their first at Wembley, they salvaged a last gasp draw. However they were still unhappy due to the manner of the opposition goal and then lost the replay.

After beating three Division Three sides, the Hammers knocked out top flight opposition in Tottenham and Coventry to reach the final, where they faced league champions Liverpool.

After normal time ended goalless the game went to extra time, with Liverpool taking the lead in controversial circumstances two minutes from the end. Alan Kennedy scored but Sammy Lee was lying injured in an offside position, obscuring the view of keeper Phil Parkes. Despite vehement protests, the goal stood.

In the final minute the Hammers were awarded a penalty when Alvin Martin's goalbound header was handled on the line. Ray Stewart converted the penalty but afterwards the normally calm John Lyall remained furious, confronting referee Clive Thomas and telling him he felt cheated.

Two and a half weeks later the replay took place at Villa Park. Paul Goddard gave the Hammers a tenth minute lead but Liverpool hit back with goals from Kenny Dalglish and Alan Hansen. West Ham were now left to concentrate on securing promotion instead.

FACT 66

1981 DIVISION TWO POINTS RECORD

West Ham cruised to promotion in 1980-81, setting a Division Two points record in the process.

There was little sign of what was to come when the Hammers lost their opening game 2-1 at home to Luton then drew two away games. However a 4-0 home win over Notts County was the start of a thirteen match unbeaten run that took them to the top of the table.

From the middle of November, West Ham remained in first place. Their Boxing Day defeat at QPR was the last of the season in the league. Despite League Cup final heartbreak against Liverpool and being taught a European lesson by Dinamo Tblisi, their league form never wavered.

West Ham played a fluid passing game that was a joy to watch, footballing their way out of the division. At least half the team were entertainers and the defence was solid, keeping 22 clean sheets. Upton Park was a fortress, with nineteen of the 21 games being won.

By the end of the season the Hammers record from 42 games was won 28, drew 10 lost 4. They were sixteen points clear of Swansea in fourth place and their total of 66 was a new record for the division.

1983
DOUBLE FIGURES

FACT **67**

The only time West Ham have scored ten goals in a competitive game was against Bury in a League Cup tie on 25th October 1983.

The Hammers had beaten the Division Four side 2-1 in the first leg, but John Lyall still named his strongest available side for the return. The fixture couldn't excite the fans though and the attendance of 10,896 was the lowest at Upton Park since 1957.

Tony Cottee opened the scoring after just two minutes but Bury had a golden chance to equalise, only for John Bramhall to hit the post with his penalty kick. Alvin Martin headed the second after seventeen minutes and Trevor Brooking got the third six minutes later.

Cottee scored two more before half-time to complete his hat-trick. However after the break there was no easing up by the Hammers. Cottee made it 6-0 on the hour and midway through the half Alan Devonshire scored from 25 yards.

The eighth goal was a penalty by Ray Stewart and after 81 minutes Brooking's lob took the score to 9-0. The tenth goal came with four minutes to left and was a low shot from Devonshire.

Despite conceding ten goals Bury's centre back Paul Hilton can't have been that bad, because five months later West Ham bought him for £100,000.

1985
FRANK LAMPARD

FACT 68

One of the club's most decorated players left at the end of 1984-85 after eighteen years there.

An Eastender who came through the West Ham academy, Frank Lampard made his debut in November 1967 when he was eighteen years old. He established himself as first choice left back that season but missed most of 1968-69 with a broken leg.

Lampard was a permanent feature of the side in the 1970s and early 1980s, helping the Hammers to two FA Cup triumphs, the finals of the League and Cup Winners Cups and one promotion.

Lampard played 660 times for the Hammers and scored 22 goals, including a famous late winner in the 1980 FA Cup semi-final against Everton. His celebration, which involved dancing around the corner flag, went into club folklore.

At the end of 1984-85 Lampard left the club on a free transfer and joined Southend, where Bobby Moore was manager. He was back at West Ham as assistant manager between 1994 and 2001. His son, also Frank, played 148 league games for the club before moving to Chelsea in 2001, having been unhappy at his father's sacking.

FACT 69

1986
HAT-TRICK AGAINST THREE DIFFERENT KEEPERS

When West Ham thrashed Newcastle 8-1 at Upton Park, Alvin Martin got a hat-trick with each of his three goals being scored against a different keeper.

Newcastle had something of a goalkeeping crisis prior to this fixture on 21st April 1986. First choice Martin Thomas was carrying a shoulder injury but with their reserve also being injured, he was forced to play through the pain.

Alvin Martin made it 1-0 after just three minutes with a close range volley. By half-time the Hammers were 4-0 up, the goals coming from Ray Stewart, Neil Orr and an own goal.

Newcastle's keeper was unable to continue in the second half and Chris Hedworth went in goal. With 25 minutes left Martin headed West Ham's fifth and Hedworth injured his collarbone whilst diving to try and save it.

Peter Beardsley volunteered to go in goal with Hedworth returning to his usual midfield position. Billy Whitehurst netted a consolation but the Hammers went on to score three in a devastating spell between the 81st and 84th minutes. Substitute Paul Goddard scored with his first touch, Frank McAvennie netted with a header and Martin completed his hat-trick from the penalty spot.

Afterwards, Martin said he didn't realise he had scored past three different keepers, only that he knew it was his first hat-trick.

1986
THE BOYS OF '86

FACT 70

West Ham's best ever league season came in 1985-86, when they finished third and had a club record winning sequence.

The Hammers were in the bottom half at the end of September, with ten games played. However a 4-1 victory over Aston Villa started a club record nine game winning run that took them to third in the table at Christmas, four points off the top.

Severe weather meant that during January and February West Ham played only three league games. By the end of March they were ten points behind Liverpool but with five games in hand. April 1986 was one of the most memorable months in the club's history, with the Hammers winning seven out of nine league games.

When the Hammers travelled to West Bromwich Albion on 3rd May they knew that they could be champions if they won their remaining two games, providing Liverpool lost their game at Chelsea. It wasn't to be though as despite the Hammers winning 3-2, Liverpool clinched the title at Stamford Bridge.

Two days later West Ham lost 3-1 at Everton, meaning they had to settle for third place. It had been an outstanding season, in which Frank McAvennie and Tony Cottee both struck twenty league goals, and one that has been talked about ever since.

1988
BILLY BONDS

FACT 71

Four years after he thought he had retired from playing, West Ham United's record appearance holder finally finished in 1988.

Billy Bonds joined the Hammers from Charlton in 1967 and immediately established himself at right back, being an ever present in 1968-69 and 1969-70. He was moved into midfield in the early 1970s, his ruggedness counterbalancing the skills of Trevor Brooking.

When Bobby Moore left in 1974 Bonds became captain, leading the Hammers to FA Cup glory the following year and the Cup Winners Cup final in 1976. He was then moved back to defence, where his ability to win possession and bring the ball forward was perfect for manager John Lyall's style of play.

In 1982-83 Bonds overtook Moore's appearance record and announced his retirement at the end of the following season. However due to an injury crisis he was persuaded to resume playing in 1984-85, but Alvin Martin was now captain. Despite being injured for all of 1985-86, Bonds got back into the side the next season even though he was now past his fortieth birthday.

Bonds finally called it a day at the end of 1987-88. He had played a total 663 league games for West Ham, scoring 48 goals.

FACT 72

1989
MCAVENNIE FAILS TO KEEP HAMMERS UP

Despite breaking the club transfer record to re-sign Frank McAvennie towards the end of 1988-89, West Ham United failed to avoid relegation.

A 4-1 home defeat to Arsenal in their fifth game saw the Hammers fall to the bottom of the table and they remained in the relegation zone all season.

On 22nd March McAvennie re-joined the club from Celtic for a record £1.1 million. However he didn't show any of the form that had made him a fans' favourite earlier in the decade. He failed to score in any of his nine league appearances between then and the end of the season.

Although McAvennie was disappointing, the Hammers did improve towards the end of the season and won four games in succession. It was too little too late though. They needed a win at title chasing Liverpool in their last game on 23rd May to stay up. Leroy Rosenior gave them a lifeline after half an hour when he cancelled out John Aldridge's strike. However Liverpool scored four times without reply in the second half to condemn West Ham to relegation.

Although the board had kept faith in John Lyall when they were relegated eleven years earlier, this time there would be no reprieve and he was sacked that summer.

FACT 73

1990 MISSING OUT ON THE PLAYOFFS

West Ham just missed out on the playoffs in 1989-90, a season that was dogged by managerial upheaval and injury.

In July 1989 the club appointed Lou Macari as manager. The Scot had led Swindon to successive promotions in 1986 and 1987 and knew all about managing in Division Two.

The Hammers were dealt a major blow when Frank McAvennie broke his leg against Stoke on the opening day of the season. This ruled him out for much of the rest of the campaign and he made only four more appearances.

There was then dissent from fans against midfielder Paul Ince, who was pictured in the newspapers with a Manchester United shirt before his transfer was announced.

Macari brought in some players that would have bright careers with the club, such as Trevor Morley, Martin Allen and Ludek Miklosko. However they struggled to gel and the Hammers were in mid table at Christmas.

In February 1990 allegations came to light that Macari had made illegal payments to players at Swindon leading to his resignation. Playing legend Billy Bonds returned to the club as manager and form improved, but a seventh place finish meant they just missed out on the playoffs.

FACT 74

1991
BACK UP

In his first full season in charge Billy Bonds led West Ham back into the top flight.

The Hammers enjoyed a 21 game unbeaten start in the league, finally losing at Barnsley on 22nd December 1990. The key to the successful campaign was a tight defence, with just 34 goals being conceded in 46 games. This was the best in the division and in contrast, they scored the least goals of any team in the top ten.

In attack Trevor Morley showed why Lou Macari had signed him the previous season and finished as the leading league scorer. Frank McAvennie also regained full fitness, scoring ten league goals to banish his injury nightmare of the season before.

West Ham were never out of the promotion places from the beginning of October. There never looked any doubt about them being promoted, especially as expansion of Division One meant three would go up automatically instead of two. However a final day 2-1 home defeat to Notts County meant they had to settle for second place with Oldham Athletic going up as champions.

FACT 75

1991 FA CUP SEMI-FINALISTS

Unlike in 1923 when West Ham were promoted and reached the FA Cup final, they failed to do this in 1991 when they lost out in the semi-final.

In the third round West Ham were embarrassed by Aldershot, who forced a 0-0 draw at Upton Park. Technically the Hammers were the away side, but the tie had been switched on safety grounds. In the replay, also at Upton Park, the Hammers made no mistake and won 6-1.

The Hammers then destroyed top flight Luton in the fourth round, winning 5-0 in a replay at Upton Park. They were then given a favourable home draw against Crewe in the next round, narrowly winning 1-0. In the quarter-final West Ham again shocked Division One opposition, beating Everton 2-1 at Upton Park.

West Ham's first FA Cup semi-final since 1980 was against Nottingham Forest at Villa Park in Birmingham. After twenty minutes Tony Gale was harshly sent off with the score at 0-0. The Hammers dreams of Wembley were shattered as Forest ran out 4-0 winners. It was their third semi-final defeat in successive seasons, having lost at the same stage in the League Cup in both 1989 and 1990.

FACT 76

1992
DOWN FROM DIVISION ONE TO DIVISION ONE

West Ham's first season back in the top flight was a disastrous one as they were relegated, missing out on a place in the new Premier League.

The Hammers didn't win until their fourth game and up until Christmas they managed to hover just above the relegation zone. A four game unbeaten run in October and November, which included a win at champions Arsenal, lifted them to fourteenth but that was as high as they would go.

Three successive defeats over the Christmas and New Year period saw the Hammers fall into the bottom three and they remained there for the rest of the season. Injuries to the previous campaign's leading scorer Tony Morley and solid defender Julian Dicks didn't help their cause.

A 2-1 defeat at Sheffield Wednesday at the end of February was the first of nine games without a win which took West Ham to the brink of relegation. A 2-0 home loss to Crystal Palace on 20th April meant that only a massive goal difference swing would save them. Relegation was finally made mathematically certain with a 1-0 defeat at Coventry in the penultimate game.

Relegation meant that for 1992-93 West Ham would again be playing in Division One following league restructuring, with the top tier becoming the Premier League.

FACT 77

1992
ANGLO ITALIAN CUP

West Ham took part in a European competition with a difference in 1992-93 when along with all other second tier clubs they entered the Anglo Italian Cup.

Back in 1975 the Hammers had faced Fiorentina in the short lived Anglo Italian Cup Winners Cup, losing both legs 1-0. Seventeen years later the format of the Anglo Italian Cup saw all second tier clubs being split into eight groups of three, with the winners moving on to an international stage.

The Hammers drew 2-2 at Bristol Rovers then beat Southend 3-0 at Upton Park. With Rovers also beating Southend by the same scoreline, it meant the a coin was tossed to determine which team went through and it landed in West Ham's favour

In the international stage the Hammers lost 2-0 away to Cremonese, then beat Reggiana 2-0 at home then won 1-0 at Cosenza. The last game was a 0-0 home draw with Pisa, meaning the Hammers finished as the second placed English team in the group, missing out on the chance of a playoff to determine who would reach the Wembley final.

Attendances in the competition were woeful, with both games in Italy attracting crowds of less than 1,000. At the end of the season the Hammers were promoted, meaning they didn't need to endure the competition the following campaign.

FACT 78

1993 UP TO THE PREMIER LEAGUE

West Ham were promoted in 1992-93, meaning they would be competing in the Premier League's second season.

The club kept faith in Billy Bonds as manager but had a mixed start to the season, losing two of the first three. They then went eight games unbeaten, a run that included some big wins; 5-1 at Bristol City, 6-0 over Sunderland at Upton Park then 4-0 at Bristol Rovers.

Clive Allen and Trevor Morley were lethal in attack, each averaging a goal every other game. In midfield, Peter Butler and Mark Robson formed a useful partnership and full back Julian Dicks contributed goals as well.

Newcastle were runaway leaders and the Hammers moved into the top two in January, but were pushed all the way by Portsmouth and Tranmere for the second automatic spot.

Promotion wasn't secured until the last day of the season when second half goals from Allen and David Speedie secured a 2-0 win at Upton Park over Cambridge United. It was enough to hold off Portsmouth on goal difference and secure a place in the Premier League where television revenues were lucrative.

FACT 79

1994
HARRY REDKNAPP TAKES OVER

In the summer of 1994 there was a managerial change at West Ham when Harry Redknapp took over team affairs.

Despite finishing twelfth and comfortably clear of the relegation zone in their first Premier League season, Billy Bonds was relieved of first team duties. He was replaced by Redknapp who had been his assistant for two seasons and played 175 times for West Ham between 1965 and 1972.

Redknapp's first season saw the Hammers avoid relegation by only five points. However he then went on to establish them as a Premier League club, rearing players from the academy such as Rio Ferdinand, Frank Lampard and Joe Cole. He also rejuvenated the careers of the likes of Stuart Pearce and Trevor Sinclair.

In 1998-99 West Ham finished fifth in the league, their second highest finish in the top flight. With such a mix of players, including some high profile stars who failed to live up to expectations, it was an exciting but unpredictable time in the club's history.

In 2001 Redknapp left the club by mutual consent, following a disappointing season compared to recent campaigns.

1995
CENTENARY TOUR

FACT 80

As part of West Ham's centenary celebrations in 1995, the club played their first ever matches in Australia.

The tour started on 19th May at the Wacca Stadium in Perth, where 10,00 fans watched a game that was anything but friendly. Both Western Australia and the Hammers had players injured in a game that finished 2-2. A shootout then took place to decide the winner, with each player having to take a thirty yard run-up. Darren Currie was unlucky for the Hammers, meaning the Australians won 5-3.

Two nights later at Olympic Park in Melbourne, West Ham were lacklustre in a 1-1 draw with Victoria, Darren Shipp scoring their goal. It was then on to Sydney to face Australia under-23's, where kickoff was delayed due to crowd congestion in the tiny 6,000 capacity stadium. John Moncur entertained the waiting crowd with a ball juggling routine and when the game began Malcolm Macpherson scored the only goal in a 1-0 win for the Hammers.

The final game of the tour was on 27th May in Brisbane, with the Australian under-23 side again the opposition. This time the Hammers were outclassed, losing 4-0.

FACT 81

1996
ALVIN MARTIN LEAVES

At the end of the 1995-96 season Alvin Martin left West Ham after 22 years at the club.

Martin joined the Hammers as a sixteen year old apprentice in 1974. He was part of the side that reached the FA Youth Cup final in 1974-75 and signed professional forms on his eighteenth birthday in 1976.

Martin made his debut in March 1978 and went on to form a successful defensive partnership with Billy Bonds. He helped the Hammers to FA Cup success in 1980 and promotion the following year. In May 1981 he made the first of his seventeen appearances for England, which included one match in the 1986 World Cup.

Despite relegations in 1989 and 1992 Martin remained loyal to West Ham, helping them back up on each occasion. By far his most famous game in a Hammers' shirt was against Newcastle in 1986, when he scored a hat-trick against three different keepers in an 8-1 win.

Martin pulled on a West Ham shirt for the last time on 5th May 1986 when he came on as an 88th minute substitute against Sheffield Wednesday. It was his 469th league appearance for the club. He was 37 years old but still had one more playing season left in him and he joined Leyton Orient.

1997
THE ONE MINUTE HAMMERS

FACT 82

The shortest playing career of a West Ham United player is arguably that of Lee Boylan, who played for just one minute towards the end of 1996-97.

Boylan came through West Ham's youth academy and was a last minute substitute against Sheffield Wednesday at Upton Park on 3rd May 1997. The Hammers were 5-1 up and there is no verification that Boylan even touched the ball.

After spending the following season on loan at Kingstonian, Boylan spent the rest of his career at non league clubs around the South East.

On 9th August 1997 David Terrier, a 24 year old French defender, came on in the last minute of a 2-1 win at Barnsley. He never played for West Ham again but did play top flight football in France.

In 2015, Alex Pike was a last minute substitute in a Europa League tie against Astra Giurgiu. As of August 2017 he is still at West Ham though so may well add to this total.

Even though these players only got on for a minute, at least they did log an appearance. In January 1999 Ezomo Iriekpen was stripped off ready to come on against Manchester United at Old Trafford, only for the referee to blow for full time. He eventually joined Swansea in 2003 without ever playing for the Hammers.

FACT 83

1997
A BETTING PLOT

On 3rd November 1997 the home game against Crystal Palace was abandoned due to floodlight failure. It was later discovered that this was due to a deliberate act of sabotage by a Far Eastern betting syndicate.

Frank Lampard scored a 65th minute equaliser for the Hammers as they came from 2-0 down in a match that was televised on a Monday night. Soon after the lights went out and the game had to be abandoned.

The following month a game between Wimbledon and Arsenal was abandoned for the same reason. However when a security guard at Charlton told a colleague that he had been bribed to make the lights go out during a game with Liverpool, the police were informed.

Investigations showed that the lights at Upton Park had been sabotaged and as such a six figure sum was paid out to a Malaysian betting syndicate. Four men were subsequently jailed for their role in the plot, which had also successfully sabotaged the Wimbledon v Arsenal game and a Derby v Wimbledon fixture in August 1997.

The postponement of the game in November did not do the Hammers any harm, as they beat Palace 4-1 the following month when it was replayed.

FACT 84

1999 INTERTOTO CUP

West Ham were one of three winners of the Intertoto Cup in 1999, qualifying for the UEFA Cup as a result.

The summer competition was much derided but a simplified format in 1999 allowed West Ham to add a competitive edge to their pre season preparations. They began on 17th July, joining at the third round stage. The Hammers beat Finnish side Jokerit 1-0 at Upton Park and then drew 1-1 in Helsinki to set up a tie with Dutch side Heerenveen.

The Hammers won both legs 1-0, although the attendance at Upton Park was just 7,485, some 4,000 less than watched the game with Jokerit. This meant that they had qualified for one of the competition's three finals.

In the first leg French side Metz won 1-0 at Upton Park, however the Hammers turned the final around away from home, winning 3-1. This meant they joined the two other final winners, Juventus and Montpellier, in the UEFA Cup.

West Ham enjoyed a comfortable 6-1 aggregate victory over Croatians Osijek in the first round, but they finally come unstuck in the next stage. After losing 2-0 in Romania to Steau Bucharest, they could only draw 0-0 at Upton Park, bowing out in their tenth competitive European game of the season.

FACT 85

1999
MANNYGATE

On 15th December 1999 West Ham thought they had edged past Aston Villa in the League Cup via a penalty shootout. However it later became apparent that they had fielded an ineligible player and the game had to be replayed.

The score was 1-1 with just a minute of the quarter-final to go when Dion Dublin scored what looked to be Villa's winner. However Paul Kitson was fouled in the box and Paulo Di Canio converted the penalty to force extra time.

There were no further goals and in the penalty shootout, Shaka Hislop saved Gareth southgate's kick to take the Hammers into the semi-final. A few days later it was found that substitute Emmanuel Omoyinmi had played for Gillingham whilst on loan there in the earlier rounds of the competition, meaning he had been ineligible to face Villa.

Manager Harry Redknapp insisted the Hammers shouldn't face any punishment as 'Manny' was only on the pitch eight minutes and touched the ball twice. However a replay was ordered, which West Ham lost 3-1.

The administrative error led to West Ham's secretary and his assistant resigning and Omoyinmi, who hadn't told Redknapp of his Gillingham appearances, never played for the club again.

FACT 86

2000
WEST HAM WIN NINE GOAL THRILLER

On 12th February 2000 West Ham were involved in one of their most entertaining games of the Premier League era. They came from 4-2 down to beat Bradford City 5-4 at Upton Park.

After just five minutes the Hammers were dealt a severe blow when keeper Shaka Hislop suffered a broken leg in a collision with Dean Saunders. Deputy Craig Forrest was on international duty, meaning teenager Stephen Bywater went in goal.

After half an hour Dean Windass headed Bradford into the lead but the Hammers struck back with goals from Trevor Sinclair and John Moncur. Just before half-time though, Moncur conceded a penalty which Peter Beagrie converted.

In the second half Bradford took advantage of Bywater's inexperience and the young keeper was at fault for two goals in quick succession that put them two goals ahead. Harry Redknapp decided there was nothing to lose and sent on Paul Kitson to join a three man attack. He soon won a penalty which was scored by Paulo di Canio.

Twenty minutes from time Joe Cole scored a brilliant solo equaliser and a great strike from Frank Lampard completed the comeback with seven minutes remaining. Afterwards Redknapp told the BBC "The supporters certainly got their money's worth today, it was a magnificent game".

FACT 87

2003 RECORD POINTS FOR RELEGATED TEAM

West Ham dropped out of the Premier League in 2002-03 having accumulated a record high of 42 points for a relegated team.

The Hammers endured a terrible start to the campaign and collected just sixteen points from their first 24 games. This included a sequence of fourteen games without a win between October and January.

Home form was awful and the Hammers didn't win at Upton Park until 29th January when they beat Blackburn 2-1. A few days later, they were beaten 3-0 at home to Liverpool and then lost 1-0 at Leeds to leave their position looking hopeless.

A 2-1 win at West Bromwich Albion on 23rd February began a run of six games without defeat, but the Hammers then lost 1-0 in a crucial game at fellow strugglers Bolton. They managed to win their next three including against Champions League hopefuls Chelsea, meaning that there was still a chance of survival on the last day.

On 11th May the Hammers travelled to Birmingham needing to better Bolton's result. They could only manage a 2-2 draw although a victory wouldn't have kept them up as Bolton beat Middlesbrough to ensure safety.

The Hammers had finished season sixteen points clear of the next placed side and no other side in Premier League history has gone down with 42 points.

FACT 88

2003 GLENN ROEDER'S BRAIN TUMOUR

West Ham's manager Glenn Roeder suffered a brain tumour towards the end to 2002-03. Although he recovered to return to work the following season, he was dismissed following a poor start.

After finishing seventh in 2001-02, Roeder was under pressure throughout the following season as the Hammers battled relegation. The 47 year old collapsed after an Easter Monday victory over Middlesbrough on 21st April 2003. After being rushed to hospital it was discovered he had suffered a brain tumour.

Trevor Brooking took over as manager for the remaining three games of the season but West Ham failed to beat the drop. Prior to the start of the new season Roeder took over team affairs again saying that he had unfinished business.

Some of the club's best players including Joe Cole and Glen Johnson left rather than play second tier football. When the Hammers lost 1-0 at relegation favourites Rotherham in their third game, the board decided to act fast and Roeder was sacked.

Alan Pardew was appointed manager and led the Hammers to the playoffs. However after beating Ipswich they lost the final to Crystal Palace, meaning another season outside the Premier League.

FACT 89

2005 PROMOTED VIA THE PLAYOFFS

After the disappointment of a year earlier, West Ham returned to the Premier League, going up after a late surge to the playoffs.

The Hammers were in the top six from the beginning of September until Christmas, but three successive defeats in January saw them slip to ninth.

In March and April the Hammers went nine games unbeaten but a 2-1 home defeat to Sunderland in their final home game put a serious dent in their playoff hopes. However the following week a 2-1 win at Watford, coupled with Reading losing at Wigan, allowed the Hammers to claim sixth place.

For the second year running the Hammers faced Ipswich in the semi-final. After a 2-2 draw at Upton Park they won 2-0 away from home to set up a final with Preston, which was played in Cardiff due to the redevelopment of Wembley.

West Ham dominated the opening stages with Tomas Repka hitting the post. Matthew Etherington, Shaun Newton and Marlon Harewood all went close but the score remained 0-0 at half-time. In the 57th minute Bobby Zamora scored and this remained all that separated the sides, meaning the Hammers were back in the Premier League.

FACT 90

2006 FA CUP HEARTBREAK

West Ham suffered heartbreak in the 2006 FA Cup final, losing on penalties after they had led in injury time.

The Hammers were underdogs against a Liverpool side that had won the Champions League the previous season. However they were 2-0 up within half an hour. Jamie Carragher scored an own goal when he turned a Lionel Scaloni cross into his own net and Dean Ashton was then first to the rebound when after Pepe Reina had saved Matthew Etherington's shot.

Djibril Cisse pulled one back for Liverpool before half-time and Steven Gerrard equalised nine minutes after the break. Then in the 64th minute Paul Konchesky crossed into the box only for the ball to deceive Reina and fly into the net. West Ham looked set to be winners of the last cup final to be played in Cardiff only for Gerrard to equalise with a superb strike in injury time.

Both sets of players were struggling in extra time and the Hammers came agonisingly close near the end when Nigel Reo-Coker's shot was turned onto the post and Marlon Harewood missed the rebound.

In the penalty shootout, only Teddy Sheringham was successful for West Ham who went down 3-1. Afterwards they were praised by Liverpool manager Rafa Benitez, who said neither side deserved to lose.

FACT 91

2006
THE OLDEST PREMIER LEAGUE SCORER

In 2006 Teddy Sheringham set the record for the oldest goalscorer since the formation of the Premier League in 1992.

Sheringham was 38 years old when he joined the Hammers from Portsmouth in 2004. He had enjoyed a glittering top flight career spanning fifteen years, appearing for Nottingham Forest, Tottenham and Manchester United.

Sheringham was the Championship's third highest scorer with twenty league goals as he helped West Ham to promotion in 2004-05. His contract was then extended by another year, taking him past his fortieth birthday.

In the summer of 2006 Sheringham was given a contract for another year and when he played for the Hammers against Charlton on 19th August, he became the oldest ever outfield player in the Premier League. He played seventeen league games that season and his goal on Boxing Day against Portsmouth again broke his record as the oldest Premier League scorer. At 40 years and 266 days, it remains a record today.

At the end of 2006-07 Sheringham was released by West Ham but he enjoyed one more season in league football, playing for Colchester in the Championship.

FACT 92

2007 CARLOS TEVEZ SAVES THE DAY

On the last day of 2006-07 Carlos Tevez scored the winning goal as West Ham escaped relegation with a win at champions Manchester United.

The Hammers went into the game needing a point to ensure safety. With Manchester United having already secured the Premier League title, Alex Ferguson rested a number of his star players. However their line-up remained a formidable one.

Despite only needing to draw, the Hammers showed a willingness to attack and Tevez had a good penalty appeal turned down. At the other end, Yossi Benayoun had to clear a shot off the line and Rob Green made a great save from John O'Shea.

In first half injury time Tevez exchanged passes with Bobby Zamora then slid the ball past Edwin van der Sar. This prompted changes from Ferguson after an hour, bringing on Ryan Giggs, Paul Scholes and Christiano Ronaldo to try and get back in the game.

Despite the home side attacking in droves, they lacked ideas and West Ham held for victory. It completed a great escape that had looked unlikely at the beginning of March, when the Hammers were bottom of the league and ten points from safety.

FACT 93

2008
GIANFRANCO ZOLA

In the summer of 2008 West Ham appointed their first overseas manager when Gianfranco Zola took over following Alan Curbishley's resignation.

Curbishley had become manager in December 2006, when Alan Pardew was sacked following a poor run of results. He led the Hammers to a respectable ninth place finish in 2007-08, but resigned after losing control of transfers.

Zola, who won eleven trophies with Chelsea, Parma and Napoli, was appointed in September 2008. It was his first club appointment, his only other managerial experience having been with Italy under 21's. However he soon became popular due to his approachability and the style with which his team played.

Carlton Cole was impressive in attack and the Hammers finished ninth in 2008-09, just two points off European qualification.

The following season was a big disappointment, with a seventeenth place finish and just 35 points. New signings failed to gel, with South African striker Benni McCarthy not scoring at all. At the end of the season Zola was sacked and went on to manage Watford, with Avram Grant taking over at Upton Park.

FACT 94

2011 RELEGATED

After finishing just one place outside the relegation zone in 2009-10, West Ham were rock bottom of the table the following season and dropped into the Championship.

After the sacking of Gianfranco Zola, the Hammers appointed Avram Grant, who had led Chelsea to the Champions League final just two years earlier, as manager.

West Ham had a disastrous start to the season, losing their first four games and managing just one win from the first fourteen. A four game unbeaten run over Christmas lifted them out of the bottom three but they were back there by February.

Successive home wins over Liverpool and Stoke, then a draw at Tottenham lifted West Ham up to seventeenth with nine games remaining. They then lost five games in a row to leave them on the brink of relegation.

On 15th May the Hammers travelled to Wigan for their penultimate game of the season. After leading 2-0 at half-time, they lost 3-2 with Wigan's winner coming in injury time. It condemned the Hammers to the drop and the club confirmed after the game that Avram Grant would leave with immediate effect.

The following week Kevin Keen was in temporary charge as Sunderland won 3-0 at Upton Park to ensure a bottom place finish for the Hammers.

FACT 95

2012
PROMOTED WITH THIRTEEN AWAY WINS

West Ham were promoted straight back to the Premier League in 2011-12. They won thirteen away games during the season, a club record, but still had to go up via the playoffs.

Now managed by Sam Allardyce, the Hammers lost their opening game at home to Cardiff, but picked up and were in the top two by the middle of October. They remained there until March, when five straight draws saw them drop out of the automatic promotion places.

Eventually West Ham finished in third place, two points behind Southampton but sixteen ahead of the fourth playoff spot. Inconsistent form at Upton Park had denied them a top two finish. They won just eleven games there, compared to thirteen on the road. This was the most away wins the club had ever achieved in a season.

In the playoff semi-final the Hammers comfortably beat Cardiff 5-0 over two legs. This set up a final at Wembley against Blackpool, who had also been relegated in 2011

Carlton Cole scored for the Hammers ten minutes before half-time, but in the 48th minute Blackpool equalised. With just three minutes remaining, Ricardo Vaz Te scored the decisive goal to ensure a top flight return at the first attempt.

2014
DYLAN TOMBIDES

FACT 96

In April 2014 striker Dylan Tombides died of cancer, leading to the retiring of his shirt number.

Tombides was born in Australia in 1994 and joined the Hammers at the age of fifteen. In 2011 he was diagnosed with cancer after a drugs test taken during the under-17 World Cup. He made a full recovery and returned to training for pre season 2012-13.

Tombides made his debut for West Ham when he came on as an 84th minute substitute in a League Cup tie against Wigan in September 2012. Three months later though the cancer had returned and he required further treatment.

Despite undergoing intense chemotherapy Tombides was able to appear in the Asian under-22 championships in January 2014. On returning to England though he was told his cancer had spread and couldn't be cured. His family were with him when he died on 18th April.

The following day the Hammers faced Crystal Palace at Upton Park. His father and brother placed a shirt with his name and number 38 at the centre circle. The squad number was then retired in his honour, something that has only been done otherwise for Bobby Moore.

In February 2015 the Dylan Tombides DT38 Foundation was launched, aimed at raising the awareness of testicular cancer.

2015
REECE OXFORD

FACT 97

The youngest player to appear for the Hammers is Reece Oxford, who was just 16 years and 198 days old when he made his debut in 2015.

Oxford joined West Ham in 2011 after being released by Tottenham. He signed his first professional contract in January 2015, a month after his sixteenth birthday and having been named captain

of England's under-17 side.

At the end of 2014-15 he was named West Ham's academy player of the year. Oxford made his first team debut on 2nd July 2015, as the Hammers made an early start to the season in the qualifying rounds of the Europa League. He played in midfield in a 3-0 home victory over Andorran minnows Lusitans.

On 9th August he played the first 79 minutes of West Ham's 2-0 at Arsenal, making him the second youngest player to start a Premier League match. He appeared in seven league games in total in 2015-16 but the following season had to settle for just two Europa League appearances before going on loan to Championship side Reading.

To help in continuing his development, Oxford was loaned to German side Borussia Monchengladbach for the 2017-18 season.

FACT 98

2015 WINNING AT ANFIELD

On 29th August 2015 West Ham finally won a league game against Liverpool at Anfield, 52 years after they had last done so.

Following a 2-1 win at Anfield in 1963, the Hammers went on a miserable run of results there,

failing to win in 42 league visits. Despite losing two of their opening three games in 2015-16, the 3,000 fans who travelled to Merseyside for this game were hopeful and in fine voice.

After just three minutes Manuel Lanzini scored for the Hammers, tapping home after a defensive lapse by Liverpool. Shortly before the half hour mark Lanzini robbed Dejan Lovren and crossed for Mark Noble to score.

Manager Slaven Bilic was constantly pacing the touchline and waving his arms about during the second half. Liverpool rarely threatened and had only two shots on target all game. However they were kicking into the Kop and one goal had the potential to change the whole atmosphere.

Seven minutes of injury time were added to prolong the agonising wait. However two minutes into it Diafra Sakho, whose treatment had been its cause, scored to put the result beyond doubt. There were joyful scenes amongst Hammers fans who stayed behind celebrating for ten minutes after the final whistle.

FACT 99 — 2016 FAREWELL TO UPTON PARK

At the end of 2015-16 West Ham said goodbye to Upton Park, their home for the past 112 years.

With capacity and potential for further development limited, the club explored various possibilities before announcing in 2013 that they had secured a lease at the 2012 Olympic Stadium, to take effect from 2016.

The final game at Upton Park was on 10th May that year against Manchester United. Before kick off the hymn 'Abide With Me' was played as the club's

greatest players faces appeared on the video screens. The last of those was Bobby Moore, who was given the greatest applause.

After taking a tenth minute lead in a cavernous atmosphere, the Hammers undeservedly trailed 2-1 with fifteen minutes remaining. However headed goals from Michail Antonio and Winston Reid gave them a deserved victory.

When the final whistle had blown, there was a 45 minute display on the pitch celebrating the history of the ground. Outside the ground in the nearby pubs, the celebrations continued long into the night. Upton Park was then sold to a developer for a housing scheme.

FACT 100

2017
THE LONDON STADIUM COMES TO LIFE

West Ham endured a difficult first season at the Olympic Stadium, which the club rebranded the London Stadium. It was not until the second to last game of the season that fans had something to really shout about.

There was phenomenal demand for seats at the new stadium, with competitive pricing meaning 52,000 season tickets were sold. Despite winning the first league game 1-0 against Bournemouth, the Hammers failed to win any of the next three matches there and were in the relegation zone in October.

Form improved over the winter but by the end of the season the Hammers had lost more games than they won at their new home. There were heavy home defeats to Arsenal, Liverpool and Manchester City, who also won an FA Cup tie 5-0.

On Friday 5th May 2017 West Ham hosted title chasing neighbours Tottenham. In an electric atmosphere, Manuel Lazzini's 65th minute strike was enough for a Hammers victory. The season had been a turbulent one but fans took delight in denting Tottenham's title hopes and it showed just what the stadium was capable of as they looked to the future.

The 100 Facts Series

Arsenal, *Steve Horton*	978-1-908724-09-0
Aston Villa, *Steve Horton*	978-1-908724-92-2
Celtic, *Steve Horton*	978-1-908724-10-6
Chelsea, *Kristian Downer*	978-1-908724-11-3
Leeds, *Steve Horton*	978-1-908724-79-3
Liverpool, *Steve Horton*	978-1-908724-13-7
Manchester City, *Steve Horton*	978-1-908724-14-4
Manchester United, *Iain McCartney*	978-1-908724-15-1
Newcastle United, *Steve Horton*	978-1-908724-16-8
Norwich City, *Steve Horton*	978-1-908724-93-9
Rangers, *David Clayton*	978-1-908724-17-5
Tottenham Hostpur, *Steve Horton*	978-1-908724-18-2
West Ham, *Steve Horton*	978-1-908724-80-9